A Perfect HOME WEDDING

Inspirations for Planning Your Special Day

KERRY EIELSON

Stewart, Tabori & Chang
NEW YORK

Published in 2000 by
Stewart, Tabori & Chang
A division of U.S. Media Holdings, Inc.
115 West 18th Street
New York, NY 10011

Distributed in Canada by
General Publishing Company Ltd.
30 Lesmill Road
Don Mills, Ontario, Canada M3B 2T6

Library of Congress Cataloging-in-Publication Data

Eielson, Kerry.
    A perfect home wedding : inspirations for planning your
special day / Kerry Eielson.
        p.   cm.
    ISBN 1-55670-928-5
        1. Weddings—Planning Handbooks, manuals, etc.
    2. Weddings—United States—Planning Handbooks,
manuals, etc. I. Title.
    HQ745.E36   2000
    395.2'2—dc21   99-35701
                                                          CIP

Printed in Singapore

10   9   8   7   6   5   4   3   2   1

First Printing

Editor: Maria Menechella
Designer: Susi Oberhelman
Contributing Editors: Laurie Orseck, Deri Reed
Produced by Smallwood & Stewart, Inc.
New York City

E N T S

INTRODUCTION

CONGRATULATIONS, on both your decision to marry and your decision to marry at home. Preparations for one of the most exciting days of your life should be thrilling. Sometimes, though, the joy gets lost in the myriad details and stress of creating a "perfect" wedding. This book aims to prevent that from happening by walking you through each step of your journey, from invitations to attire, from flowers to music. Profiles of eight real-life home weddings will show you the range of what is possible with a little foresight and imagination, and a resource guide will point you to the best designers, planners, and stylists in the country to help you along the way.

We hope you'll turn to *A Perfect Home Wedding* for inspiration and encouragement, using it as adviser and checklist, so that every part of this process is a pleasure. After all, the hard part—finding the love of your life—is over.

The Decision to MARRY AT HOME

THIS IS IT. TWO PEOPLE are about to embark on the adventure of a lifetime. They will consecrate their union in the presence of relatives and friends who have played a formative role in their lives. They may choose to do so in a setting as rich with meaning and memories as those close relationships and decide to marry at home. A home wedding is not only an expression of the couple's love for each other, but also a reflection of all those things that make them who they are—their family histories, personalities, and lifestyles. ✦

All Things Considered

A HOME WEDDING PRESENTS A COUPLE with a unique opportunity to create an exceptional moment in their lives exactly as they want it to be. It is their chance to put a truly personal stamp on every aspect of the event, to express individual perspectives and tastes. "A home wedding is an inviting setting that relaxes people, that lets the focus be on the celebration of a new union," says Christopher Robbins of Robbins and Wolfe Eventeurs in New York City.

But the home wedding is not the simple, idyllic arrangement it may seem at first glance. It may require more planning—and sometimes even more expense—than more formal options outside the home. Unlike events held at hotels or other conventional sites, where many functions are handled by the establishment and expenses are included in one overall price, everything involved in the home wedding is à la carte. The cost—custom menu; wait staff (including bartenders); music; flowers; table, chair, china, glassware, silverware, and linens rentals; licenses, valets and, if necessary, tents—can add up to more than the cost of renting a space and services.

It also adds up to a lot of details to manage, and a lot of wear and tear on home and property. If you envision the days before a wedding to be serene, think again: There may be wedding professionals underfoot for as many as five days before. There will be a large number of people in the house and on the grounds, both before and during the wedding. Tents are generally pitched three days in advance of the event. Out-of-town guests will want to visit, even if they are staying elsewhere. A florist or designer will probably need several days to decorate. If yours is a do-it-yourself affair, there may be fewer professionals around, but you will still need friends and family to help shoulder the responsibilities. Even if it's a small gathering, there is always the chance of some damage, most likely broken dishes and food stains. "Take tablecloths, for example," says wedding designer

Clockwise from top left: An informal portrait just before the wedding marks the ceremony's official beginning. Comfortable, well-lit space for the wedding party to dress in is a must. For centerpieces, simple glass bowls are filled with rich bouquets of spring flowers. The new couple leads off the first dance. The harpist prepares to sound the earliest notes of welcome.

Anthony Todd. "They come back from the most elegant home weddings looking as if no one had a fork or a knife—which is a good sign. It means people had a great time." It takes another day after the big event to dismantle the tent, return the rentals, and send people off.

"There's much more involved in the planning," admits New York City party consultant Elizabeth Allen. "But in the long run, it can be so incredibly special to have your wedding in a place that you are familiar with, that is linked to your past, friends, and family." As Robbins points out, "It doesn't have to be so serious. Have a sense of humor; have a sense of wonder. Even if it's pouring outside and muddy in the tent, you've found the person you'll share the rest of your life with."

A home wedding provides the perfect excuse to do renovations, make repairs that have been put off, or give the house a fresh coat of paint. If these improvements aren't in your budget, there are other ways to hide flaws. Todd recommends drawing attention away from imperfections: "This is one instance where it's a good idea to overlook the details. Don't worry about, or try to hide, the architectural flaws of the house. If anything, seduce guests' eyes away with a superb arrangement."

The first logistical consideration is space. Will you be hosting the ceremony and the reception, or just the reception? Will the event be indoors? If so, look at the layout of the house as if it were filled with tables (even if you're not having a sit-down dinner, you'll need room for the buffet and cabaret tables) and guests. Is there room in the kitchen for a caterer? What kind of meal can be prepared there for the number of guests invited? Think about the accessibility to exits and other rooms. Visualize fifty people in the room you're planning to use: Will it feel like a subway car at rush hour? Anticipate bottlenecks that may be created between the bathroom and the reception area. Be absolutely certain you have ample ventilation, a place where furniture can be stored, and space for an aisle and ceremonial focal point. You may decide to do a stand-up ceremony because it requires less space; you may decide on cabaret seating

Clockwise from top left: The route to the ceremony site should be safe and accessible. Downtime for a bride is spent relaxing with her flower girls. Finally dressed, a wedding party smiles wide for the photographer. Table settings are completed while the ceremony is going on. Hundreds of flickering candles accompany a serenade for the bride and groom.

and a buffet meal for the same reason. Linda Matzkin of Hopple Popple Event Planners in Boston says, "When a couple comes to me to do a home wedding, I always ask them if I can come over and play. We need to get in there to get a sense of the setting and the dimensions, to feel our way around. If it looks like there isn't good accessibility to the kitchen for the caterers, or for the guests from one part of the room to another, I suggest a garden or tent wedding."

For an outdoor ceremony and reception, lawns, gardens, terraces, and pools provide a lovely backdrop. Some people even plant a year in advance, from tulips in their flower bed to wildflowers on the back lawn. While having the event outside solves some problems and has aesthetic rewards, it, too, requires serious planning. Preparations need to be made for lighting and electrical demands. Call your local city hall to see if there are ordinances regarding tents, from limitations on their size to the amount of time they can be left in place. Find out if there are any noise or parking restrictions. Ask your fire department about safety precautions. Check your homeowner's insurance for coverage for any accidents that could occur while setting up, during the party, or while people are driving home; if coverage

An elegant wedding "picnic" is styled with lush rustic centerpieces and wicker bread baskets (below left). Outdoor weddings can be formal or informal, depending on the number of guests, the style of the home, and the attire stipulated on the invitation. A grand home (below center) offers the perfect stage for a black-tie event. Sometimes nature provides the opulence. In an outdoor ceremony (below right), the only aesthetic element is a rich backdrop of trees.

isn't provided, take out a rider to cover liability for those situations. If you have guests with special needs, make accommodations for them, including rest room facilities, transportation to and from the event, a ramp to the house, or a solid walkway.

While it may be a joy for you to have your wedding in your back-yard, it might not be for your neighbors. Most wedding planners suggest writing a note informing them of your plans and apologizing for any inconvenience the noise and traffic might cause them; tucking the note into a basket of cookies is a gracious added touch. Parking is always a challenge for home weddings. If guests are going to be parking on the street, appoint someone to make sure that neighbors can still get in and out of their driveways. Valets can be hired or a friend designated to shuttle guests to and from a nearby church or school with an available lot. Guests shouldn't have to walk a mile in their party shoes. Valets can also pick them up at hotels or train stations to reduce the number of cars near the property.

Smaller weddings can take place entirely within one room. Because space was at such a premium, this couple opted not to include bridesmaids and groomsmen (above left). After the ceremony, guests adjourned to a small hallway for the receiving line so caterers could bring in tables and chairs for the reception (above right).

The Right Style

"ONE REASON TO HAVE A HOME WEDDING is to reflect the style of the bride and groom," says Boston planner Linda Matzkin. Your taste, rather than the surroundings, are first and foremost in determining whether this will be a formal or informal affair, whether it will be morning, noon, or night, buffet or sit-down, peonies or pansies, barbecued pork or filet of sole. You are not influenced by the colors and decor of the rented space, or restrained by rigid scheduling. Even if you're working with a limited budget, there are still innovative ways to create the wedding of your dreams.

Sculptural centerpieces of oranges echo the manicured landscaping and tropical climate of an outdoor reception (below left). A striped tent (below right) creates the feeling of a festival—especially with the tent sides drawn up. Unlike indoor weddings, tent affairs can be far grander than the style of the house itself. One dramatic reception featured more than twenty tables with lavish, soaring centerpieces (opposite).

When deciding how formal you want your wedding to be, keep in mind how many guests you'd like to invite, the time of day you want to have the ceremony, and where you would like to hold it. Generally, the later the affair, the more formal it can be. Nighttime events, with their special lighting and candles, are dramatic in a way that a breakfast simply isn't. Daytime is considered more casual than evening, outdoors more casual than indoors. Garden parties are by their very nature less formal. But that's not to say that

a formal afternoon event in a rustic setting cannot work beautifully: A Champagne garden reception with a harpist can be far more elegant—and less expensive—than a roast beef luncheon in a hotel.

Approaching your wedding as you do other entertaining at home will provide the most natural results and the most pleasure. More than anything else, your goal should be to make your guests feel at home. This is an extraordinarily special occasion, a chance for you to bring out your family's best china, decorate the house and grounds, indulge in hiring an excellent caterer, and find the perfect

A formal, clean aesthetic showcases fine silver and a balance of tall, thin tapers and low arrangements (opposite). With breathtaking windows and high ceilings (above left), a few garlands are all that's needed for an intimate home wedding. A chuppah, composed of a single swath of white cloth attached to the garlanded poles (above center), frames the ceremony. An immaculately dressed table (above right) can stand on its own.

musical accompaniment. If you're planning a glamorous affair, go all out. If you're planning a smaller, more intimate gathering, choose the best of everything on a smaller scale.

Though anything is possible, it makes sense to extend the feel of the home to the decorations and rentals. Design floral arrangements so they echo the landscaping of your home. Incorporate colors from the garden and house into the decor of the party. Use personal serving dishes and an eclectic collection of colorful containers for centerpieces. Use souvenirs from your travels to set your table—textiles from India used as tablecloths, porcelain vases from Portugal for flowers. If you're a garden lover, place a potted plant or herb at each setting as a party favor, or a single stem of different flowers for each centerpiece. If you live in a rustic setting, don't be afraid to use sunflowers or other bold botanicals alongside your family's best crystal; the contrast alone will say something about who you are.

White, of course, is the traditional color of weddings. Amazingly versatile, it can strike a crisp, summery, and informal chord as well as an elegant one. It has an entirely different effect on small cabaret tables with cotton slipcovered garden chairs and galvanized buckets of tulips than it does with linen, gold-backed ballroom chairs, white roses, and tall tapers. Overall, it's a calming, welcome presence in any setting.

But many designers today are encouraging the use of color at home. "White on white weddings can be beautiful, but everyone knows that, and there are so many of them now," says wedding designer Todd. "Color brings back the element of fun that is so important to a wedding. Do the unexpected." Don't be afraid to use jewel tones for drama and excitement—emerald greens, ruby reds, sapphire blues. Consider extravagant holiday color combinations of red and gold. Contrary to what you might think, no combination of colors is inappropriate as long as it's part of a coherent theme. A color

A home wedding characterized by vivid color, clockwise from top left: A crystal bowl filled with flowers picked from the garden becomes the table's focal point. Chilled white wine awaits thirsty guests. A cheerful feel is achieved with colorful tablecloths collected by the bridal couple on their travels to Asia, earthy bursts of sunflowers nestled in moss, and red votive candles. Galvanized buckets stuffed with long-stemmed roses are an indulgent accent. Tablecloths that extend to the ground give the otherwise casual look an elegance. Every party gets a touch of extravagance from an abundance of champagne.

story could echo the surroundings or find a common thread in the fabric used. For a wedding in a field of grapevines, a tent was dressed in gorgeous rich silks of olive green, blood red, and gold. The accents added even more depth to the palette's range: tent poles wrapped in deep aqua silks and topped with sunflowers. On the tables were rust and tangerine silk cloths, along with amber, plum, and gold glass. What held this riot of color together was the fact that all the tones were rich but dusty, and all conveyed a sense of revelry and abandon appropriate in a vineyard.

Dozens of fanciful paper lanterns strung over a pool bounce about in the afternoon breeze (opposite). Cabaret tables and chairs with white cotton tablecloths and slipcovers have a polished but casual effect (below left). Tiny potted plants act both as decorative accents and as wedding favors to be added to guests' gardens after the celebration. A uniformly set banquet table and special glassware combine formal and informal (below right).

HIRING A *Wedding Planner*

A DO-IT-YOURSELF home wedding is feasible, but those who prefer to (and can afford to) may opt to leave the planning and details to someone else. A wedding planner can act as the liaison with other professionals involved in your wedding arrangements. A good planner will make the experience a dream for you, so it is essential to find one who has an affinity for you, your style, and your way of doing things. He or she will listen carefully to your ideas and be realistic about what can be accomplished within your budget. Several wedding planners offered the following suggestions for finding the right person.

❖ There is nothing better than a personal referral. Ask your friends, relatives, and other professionals such as florists and bridal boutique owners whose taste is similar to yours.

❖ Interview more than one planner, get more than one bid, and do so at least six to nine months before the wedding.

❖ Decide how involved you want the planner to be. Do you want a full-service operation that takes charge of every detail from invitations to trash removal, or someone who is simply there to help carry out decisions?

❖ Find out if the planner charges a flat fee, an hourly fee, or a percentage of the fees charged by the florist, band, caterer, etc.

If you're looking for someone who will be involved in every step of the process, you may get the most for your money with one who charges a flat fee. In addition, you may have more control over the choice of vendors.

❖ When interviewing wedding consultants (or people who have used them), be sure to ask the following questions:

Is there anything they won't do?

Will they understand and cater to your vision? Can they represent and reflect your taste?

Are they easy to work with?

Are they accessible for meetings with vendors?

Do they return your calls promptly?

Do they respect your budget?

Do they work only with certain vendors, or can you bring in your own?

Do they assist in negotiations and take the time to navigate through proposals, explaining where it's possible to cut costs?

Will they supply a detailed schedule of the days leading up to the event, and of the day itself?

Will they stay until the very end of the affair?

Invitations and Programs

THE INVITATION IS THE first element of a wedding that guests see, and it sets the tone for the event. "The quality of the invitation has even been said to affect the quality of the gifts a couple will receive," claims Mary Griffin, etiquette specialist at Cranes. "Very nice invitations let guests know this will be a very special occasion, and indicate its formality, saying, 'This is going to be an exquisite affair.' People buy gifts accordingly." The reply card, accommodation card, and map (often printed together) indicate what else guests can expect—how they should dress, if the event is outside or inside, and if they will need to travel or make hotel arrangements.

Traditionally, invitations have been formal: black or dark gray ink, embossed print-ing, white or ecru paper five by seven inches and side-folded, standardized wording ("Mr. and Mrs. Jones request the pleasure of your company at the marriage of their daughter . . .").

Invitations for weddings are no longer limited to black engraving on white paper. Lavender ink and envelopes using flowers and illustrations as decorative touches (below left) convey the tone of a summer garden wedding. Brightly colored notecards have a contemporary flair (below center). Professional calligraphy and a trail of ribbon add romance to a stylish invitation (below right).

Today, the range of invitation formats and language is enormous. "People still want to be proper, but they want their invitation and their wedding to be specific to them, and memorable in that way," explains Violet Brandywine at Kate's Paperie in New York City. Many couples eschew formal invitations and choose to have ones that complement an element of their wedding: using blue ink for a wedding near the water, for example, or a ladies' slippers illustration for New England nuptials. Some choose colorful handmade paper in lieu of machine-pressed paper, or incorporate lace overlays, a touch of ribbon, or crushed flowers; others hand-illustrate invitations and use custom-designed wax seals.

Programs serve as a guide to the ceremony, introduce guests to the wedding party, and provide a place for the bride and groom to thank friends and family. They are often less formal than invitations and so are ideal candidates for creative personal expression.

One bride and groom illustrated their program with drawings of themselves as children (below left); satin ribbon gives them a dressy finish. Programs printed with the initials of the bride and groom and tied with gauzy ribbon take their place next to stacks of velvet yarmulkes (below right). Programs with ribbons or flowers attached should be carefully stacked before the ceremony (opposite).

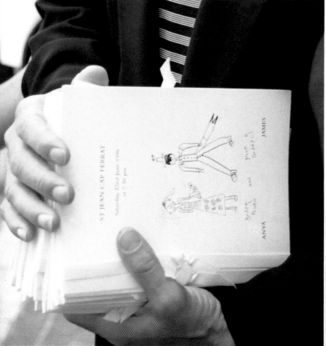

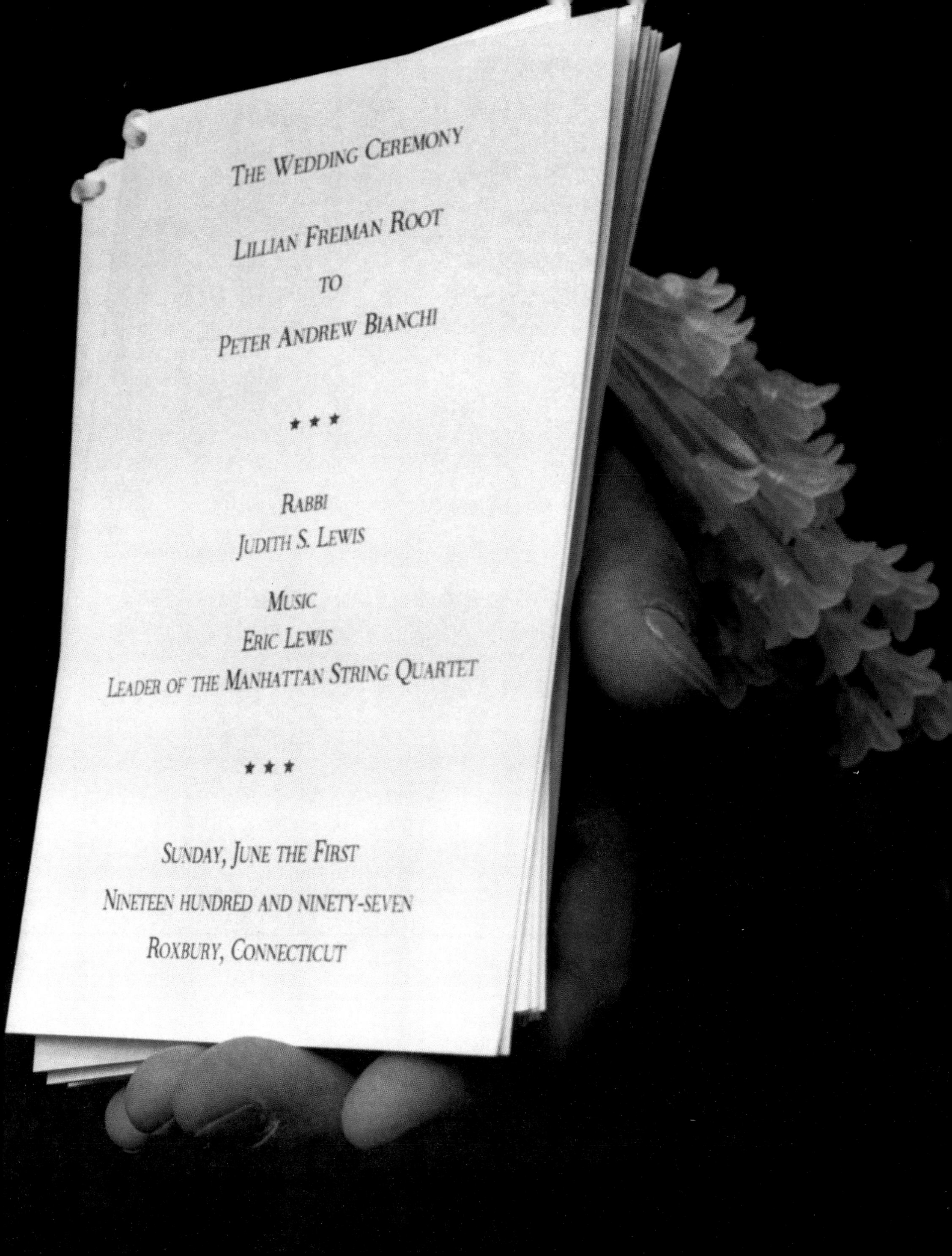

THE WEDDING CEREMONY

LILLIAN FREIMAN ROOT

TO

PETER ANDREW BIANCHI

★ ★ ★

RABBI
JUDITH S. LEWIS

MUSIC
ERIC LEWIS
LEADER OF THE MANHATTAN STRING QUARTET

★ ★ ★

SUNDAY, JUNE THE FIRST

NINETEEN HUNDRED AND NINETY-SEVEN

ROXBURY, CONNECTICUT

Setting THE STAGE

IT'S OFFICIAL. YOU'RE going to be married at home. Though such a decision may feel like it will simplify your life, don't be deceived: Planning even a relatively small wedding at home can feel like you're directing a Broadway play! Consider the logistics. Once a location is chosen, a "set" must be constructed, complete with furniture and "props." Then come "costumes," music, and lighting. Throw in a diva (every family has one) and the analogy is complete. The difference, of course, is that this production is for real, and for life. The good news is that planning *will* make it happen. ❖

Outmaneuvering the Weather

SUN-DRENCHED, SWELTERINGLY HOT, tempestuous, plain drizzly—there are of course no guarantees when it comes to the weather. But every wedding, indoors or out, can be a success, regardless of the elements—as long as a backup plan exists, people are flexible, and attitudes remain upbeat. "I've seen weddings where it rained so hard all you could hear was thrumming on the roof," says event planner Christopher Robbins. "But people had a terrific time. Over and over again, I've seen guests rise to the occasion."

Guests rush to shelter a bride from a sudden shower and keep her skirts from touching the ground (opposite)— a vision no less memorable than a day of endless sun. Tent ceremonies are always elegant, rain or shine; the elements are visible but can't interfere (below).

Often the weather's effect is psychological as well as logistical. If feet feel wet, the bride looks upset, and her mother seems harried, guests are less likely to forget that it's raining on their parade. Have contingency equipment in place: Buy inexpensive mats or runners, and even large rugs from home supply stores, and place them over portable walkways and floors to keep feet dry. If you don't have a canopy covering the walk from the parking area to the tent or the house, equip valets with large umbrellas to escort people inside. Create a place where guests can check their coats and change into dry shoes. Provide lots of umbrella holders and have extra umbrellas on hand to give to departing guests. "Rain isn't the only issue," points out

Even a brief wait and short ceremony can be grueling in the middle of the day. Lightweight paper parasols protect guests from the sun's withering rays, serve as conversation pieces, and are memorable favors to take home.

consultant Peter Helburn. "Direct sunlight is, too." A stylish way to deal with this is to place umbrellas over guests' chairs or give each guest a parasol or a large, white golf umbrella to use for protection. And keep in

Little did this couple know that the large torches outside their party tent would offer more than a theatrical visual effect. During a storm, once the skies darkened, the torches were necessary to light the way from ceremony to reception.

mind that a sunny day after a night of rain is often a buggy day. Plan to have enough citronella candles and tiki torches as defense against insects. For added insurance, bomb the area a few hours before the ceremony and place canisters of bug spray—tied with ribbon, of course—all around the site.

Sometimes the best defense against a fickle climate is to reserve a tent as a backup plan in case of really unbearable weather. It can be outfitted with heaters and air conditioners.

Pitching Your Tent

LOOK AT THE TENT AS IF IT WERE a room in your house. Keith Waters of J. G. Willis, Inc. in Boston advises that the goal should be to make the space comfortable enough to live in. That includes lighting, flooring, and temperature control. Once outfitted, a tent can be as sturdy and serviceable as a building. If you want to have the reception in your home but there simply isn't enough space, pitching a tent as an extension to

your house directly outside the front or back door is a way to welcome guests without making it seem like there are two parties going on.

Making an extra tent available to caterers for their service station and another one to guests before and after the festivities will mean less wear and tear in the house and more privacy and comfort for guests. Furnish a small tent with a vanity, a clothes rack, a small table, and chairs to serve as a guest room for out-of-towners

A small pole tent serves as a dressing room for a bridal party (above left); during the reception, guests with small children use it for much-needed breaks. Plush square stools and white balloons turn a tent (above right) into a cosmopolitan cocktail area for a waterfront wedding. A small striped century tent (opposite) showcases the wedding cake and protects it from heat.

to relax in after a long journey, an oasis for people fatigued by all the fun, a changing area for the bride and bridesmaids, or a playroom for children.

A tent should be mounted about three days before the wedding to allow for adjustments and decorations. Where it is pitched depends on the land. Check the site in the months before the event. Is there a wet spot on the lawn after rains? Are there wind tunnels? Is the yard on a slope? Are there obstructions such as tree limbs that can be removed, or power lines and septic systems that can't? A graceful tent set in the midst of a vast meadow is a beautiful sight, but not always practical. Electrical power, water supplies, and rest rooms need to be immediately accessible at every wedding, and in the event of inclement weather, the leisurely walk from the field may become a race through rain and mud.

Robert Slavik of Abbey Party Rents in Dallas suggests that reservations be made for large tents with extensive decorations at least three months in advance. "If you reserve, you'll get a better tent. Otherwise, you might wind up with leftovers," he notes. If the tent is just your fallback position in case of bad weather, Slavik advises, "book the tent no matter what. If the weather is beautiful and there is no sign of rain, you can cancel a few days ahead." (Be sure to find out the time limit on cancellations, or be prepared to forfeit part of your deposit as a payment for a sunny day.) Large companies will help with features such as climate control, lighting, and decorating. They will also have people on hand in the event that the weather changes, necessitating accommodations in the tent. If you're renting from a smaller company, work with a florist or caterer with extensive experience to troubleshoot for you.

If your budget is modest, consider adding one strong architectural or design element to a basic tent. A white dance floor will expand the feeling of interior space; an elaborate chandelier will draw the eye up and act as a witty foil for the canvas structure. Tent poles should always be covered, either with flowers, fruits or vegetables or with ribbon, tulle, or fabric. The entrance should be marked with flowers as well, both on the exterior and the inside. Once the tent has been erected, install your lighting and test it at the time of the reception to be sure it is effective.

A clear-top tent (opposite) is intended for night use to showcase the sky. Tiny bee lights strung along the ceiling add to the starry effect. With such a solid tent construction, there is no worry about rain; its sound on the roof only adds to the magical feeling within.

TENT *Fundamentals*

- Party tents are made of vinyl canvas, which can withstand repeated folding, hauling, washing, pitching, and dismounting. Some are heat-sealed, with three layers to keep the environment warmer or cooler. Anchors are made of wood or steel.

- The most basic and inexpensive variety, pole tents have poles for support in the center and/or around the perimeter. Because they require staking, they don't work on asphalt or cement.

- Frame tents include poles around the periphery, so there is no obstruction of view. All very large tents are of this kind because of their sturdiness. They cost almost twice that of pole tents.

- Clear-top tents are frame tents with transparent ceilings. Avoid this model for a hot summer day unless you have serious air conditioning—it creates a greenhouse effect and often fogs up. Cost: almost double that of a standard frame tent.

- Century tents are distinguished by one or more conical peaks and can be constructed from either frame tents or pole tents.

- Tent sides, known as sidewalls, are available in solid models; solid models with windows; solid with real French doors; or completely clear and distortion-free, with Velcro openings every twenty feet for ventilation.

  Note: Order sides regardless of the forecast; they can be tied up if the sun shines or brought down in the event of summer squalls or evening chills—but don't leave them down unless necessary; they tend to look less festive.

- Wooden stakes with duckbill anchors work best for sand or moist earth; the wood expands so the stake won't slide out. Steel stakes are used for asphalt, anchors for cement.

- Heaters, heat lamps, and air conditioning can be installed in all kinds of tents. Have an electrician check the power supply and order a generator if necessary.

- Climate controls should be installed behind the band so the noise is drowned out. They should be activated about an hour before guests arrive.

- A tent's saturation point is reached after two days of rain. If your tent becomes soaked, strategically place towels around the floor line and designate someone to wipe down the tent sides when necessary.

- The tent should be fireproof and insured; if it is damaged in a storm, or a worker is injured during set-up, you want to make sure this isn't the homeowner's liability.

Divine Designs

THE RIGHT TRIMMINGS CONVEY a spirit of celebration. No corner should be ignored. When deciding where to place the most dramatic decorative elements—great arrangements in urns or elaborate festoons of fabric and flowers—think of how your guests will be circulating through the house or reception area. Mark the entrance to your home with wreaths and garlands. Embellish columns and tent poles with greenery, tulle, large bows, and potted plants. Use plantings from your garden; vines, fruits and vegetables, and even rocks can be incorporated to create harmony inside and out. If you're a New Englander, decorate with corn cobs, husks, buckets of pumpkins, and gourds. If you live near the ocean, put out small wooden boats and scatter shells around them. Or add bows that echo an element of your gown.

There are many ways to turn obstructions such as tent poles into decorative accents. A hanging plant seduces the eye away from the tent structure and adds a homey touch (below left). Tall grasses clustered around tent poles topped with dense bunches of fresh vegetables (below center) establish the harvest theme of an autumn wedding. A wreath of sunflowers encircles a column at an entrance (below right). Sideless tents can be bordered with tall arrangements of bushy plants like hydrangea (opposite).

Beyond the standard swags, flowers, and twinkle lights, the options for a fantastic tent interior are endless. Create one with a Tibetan flavor, an overgrown pergola, a fabric pavilion, a disco, or an elegant living room. It's not necessary to hire a professional if you and your friends have the time, talent, and initiative to do it yourself. Just think carefully before following short-lived decorating trends; the feel of your wedding should be personal and timeless.

Gossamer cloth liners (provided by the rental company) pulled along the ceiling in one generous swath or gathered into pleats give the interior a soft, billowy look and hide tent imperfections. Poles can be camouflaged with a twist of small white lights under a loose wrap of shimmer-sheer material, or with two panels of straight sheer cloth or silk shantung on either side. Chandeliers instantly create a ballroom look. Don't underestimate the power of a fresh coat of white spray paint on poles (ask the rental company). Consider renting, borrowing, or buying furniture from thrift stores, friends, advertising stylists, and theater companies.

At the entrance to a tented reception (opposite), a dramatic arrangement of flowers in a sculptural urn, surrounded by candles and more flowers, steals the show. Smaller, subtler displays can also be charming. Floral notes on each aisle chair (above left) mark the bride's path. Pots of topiaries and flowers grace the entrance to another wedding walkway (above right).

Fashioning the Table

MANY WEDDING PLANNERS SUGGEST that if you're going to focus on only one decorative aspect of your reception, it should be the tables. From a wedding breakfast to a late-night supper, they can be personalized to your taste. Cabaret seating—smaller cocktail tables that seat three or four for a buffet meal—is the most casual. No seat assignments are necessary; guests eat, mingle, and dance in a staggered manner rather than in any organized fashion. Round dinner tables that seat six to eight are for small, slightly more formal weddings. The largest tables, which seat ten, and long banquet tables are used for more elaborate events.

Because rented tables aren't always in perfect condition, linens are an important consideration. The typical wedding tablecloth is white, though using linens in other colors is a great way to add flair without breaking the bank: A pretty yellow linen with ivory napkins makes for a cheerful summer luncheon; navy blue looks regal; a different color for every table is inventive and very informal.

Regardless of table size or wedding style, Christopher Robbins advises using cloths that go to the floor. "Long tablecloths hide the ugly legs of rental tables and make them feel more substantial. They can be found on the Internet, and airshipped to you for a reasonable price."

Even the choice of chairs can transform the atmosphere of a gala or a garden party. High-backed gold-painted ballroom chairs are the most formal; simple wooden folding chairs are perfect for an outdoor "picnic" party. To go for something fanciful, paint chairs in different colors, or use a motley selection of chairs from thrift stores. Metal folding chairs can be pretty grim; transform them with slipcovers. On any chair, color from the wedding scheme

Clockwise from top left: A table with everything on it conveys abundance and indulgence as large floral arrangements take center stage; a tulle swag covers the linen cloth; even the napkins are tied with long, luxurious strands of ribbon. A much simpler table, with a less extensive setting and smaller bouquets, has a quieter effect. A long table is dramatic enough that it doesn't need much in the way of decoration—a row of short white candles suffices. The spare, sparkling elegance of silver and glass is appropriate for a small, yet still formal, affair; the silver-framed place markers double as wedding souvenirs for guests to take home.

can be brought in with sashes, cushions, or slipcovers, from formal sateen to practical poly-cotton to casual canvas.

If you're having a small wedding, by all means take out the family china. For larger weddings, where things are more likely to get broken, it's best to go with rented plates and glasses.

Seat markers should be an attractive part of any table setting. Besides the traditional table numbers and name cards, there are any number of

clever and personal ways to assign guests to their seats. One bride, a ceramic artist, selected a different vase for each table, then drew illustrations of the vases next to each person's name on the seating plan; guests matched the vases to find out where they sat. Another bride ordered a colorfully frosted cookie with each guest's name as a delicious seating device.

Table numbers and seat assignments should be considered part of the decor. For a formal tabletop, conventional place cards with hand-lettered names are placed at each seat (opposite). A small picture frame discreetly denotes the table number (above left). An alternative to a seat card, a framed picture with the seat assignment announced underneath becomes a personal gift (above right).

Seating Tactics and Tact

MAKING THE MOST of the room you've chosen is a feat of logic not unlike a military maneuver. Start by drawing up a floor plan, including the location of the band, exits, catering stations, buffet, bathrooms, and best views. Then imagine yourself as a guest and situate the tables in a way that would allow for the best flow. Make sure the focus of the room is the bride and groom.

Devising a seating plan comes next. Do you want to assign just tables but not specific seats? Should you seat families and friends together, or mix it up? (The latter can be more interesting in the long run.)

There are two scenarios for placement of family and attendants. In the more common arrangement, the head table consists of the couple, their parents and grandparents, and the officiant. The wedding party is at tables throughout the room. Alternatively, the wedding party is at the head table, and parents, grandparents, and friends are at a "second" head table. Families with small children and elderly relatives might prefer sitting near the exits, away from the band.

One couple chose an unconventional medium—plant markers—as a witty way to deal with table assignments (above left). The wedding guest book is positioned nearby. Some seating plans require several drafts (above right). A seating plan mounted at the entrance to the tent (opposite) means fewer elements on the tables—and more money in the budget for other concerns.

SEATING ARRANGEMENT

Mr. & Mrs. Howard Barter	5		Mr. & Mrs. Fredrick Martin	13
Mr. George Bianchi	1		Ms. Christina Maturi & Guest	10
Mr. & Mrs. Kevin Booker	14		Mr. Harold Maturi & Guest	16
Mrs. A.J. Butler	14		Mr. & Mrs. Bruce McLaughlin	7
Mr. Lawrence Butler			Mr. & Mrs. Douglas McLaughlin	5
Mr. & Mrs. William Campbell	13		Mr. Justin McLaughlin	6
Mr. & Mrs. David Crouch	12		Sister Cora McLaughlin & Guest	14
Mr. Everette Crouch, Jr.	12		Ms. Madelaine McQuillan	14
Mr. & Mrs. Timothy Currier	15		Mr. Patrick McQuillan	1
Mr. & Mrs. Clarence Deane	12		Mr. & Mrs. William McQuillan	12
Mr. & Mrs. Michael Delany	5		Mr. & Mrs. David Newtown	3
Ms. Sara Dorman	6		Ms. Betsy Nickerson	4
Mr. & Mrs. Edward English	10		Mr. & Mrs. Thomas Norelli	2
Mr. & Mrs. Franklin Freeman	13		Mr. & Mrs. T. O'Grady	1
Mr. & Mrs. Woody Freeman	2		Mr. Russell Olsen	15
Mrs. Richard Frock	3		Ms. Kristen O'Reilly & Guest	10
Ms. Meg Garrity	10		Mr. & Mrs. Thomas Parnell	11
Ms. Diana Gray	1		(with Christopher & Amy)	
Mr. & Mrs. David Gray	7		Mr. & Mrs. Vincent Pinto	16
Mr. Peter Gray and Guest	6		Mr. & Mrs. Daniel Ryan	16
Mr. & Mrs. Gary Harmon	4		Miss Sarah Rosenbach	9
Mr. & Mrs. Michael Harrington	8		Mr. & Mrs. Woody Rosenbach	9
Ms. Shannon Hicks	3		Mr. & Mrs. Thomas Shadler	15
Mr. & Mrs. J.P. Hughes	1		Mr. & Mrs. William Shannon	6
Ms. Brenda Hrostek	3		Mr. G.E.B. Slocum	5
Mr. & Mrs. Christopher Kachur	8		Mr. & Mrs. Thomas Slocum	5
Mr. & Mrs. Bryan Kachur	6		Mr. Evan Smith	10
Ms. Beverly Kellas & Guest	11		Miss Holly Brook Smith	11
Mr. Conn Kelly	3		Mr. & Mrs. M. Brooke Smith	10
Mr. & Mrs. Patrick Kelly	12		Mr. Michael Smith	7
Mr. & Mrs. Red Kelly	4		Mrs. N. Brooke Smith	7
Mr. & Mrs. Leo Ketter	4		Mr. & Mrs. Nathaniel Smith	8
Mr. Michael Kirk & Guest	2		Ms. Shirley Smith	7
Mr. & Mrs. Howard Kleiger	16		Ms. Marge Smith	11
Mr. Michael Llodra & Guest	1		Mr. Joseph Ruszeski	7
Mr. & Mrs. Robert Llodra	13		Mr. & Mrs. Charles Thermer	9
Miss Carol Lucas	4		(with Sarah & Jonathan)	
Mr. Peter van Colen & Guest	3		Mr. Michael Walsh	14
Mr. Thomas Warzecha	6		Mr. Peter Wilson	15

Flowers and More Flowers

WEDDINGS AND FLOWERS make a happy marriage. "There's something of the fairy tale in flowers," says Kristine Ellis of Kristine Fleurs in New York City. "Something innocent, romantic, and otherwordly, in part due to the effect of their scent." Those scents can have a magical effect on the tone of the ceremony and party.

Floral basics include bouquets for the bride and bridesmaids; boutonnieres for the groomsmen and fathers; corsages for the mothers and grandmothers; and decorations for the setting. Give something playful to the flower girl, such as a wreath of baby roses or Queen Anne's lace, a basket with loose petals, or a garland of trailing greenery to mark the path of the bride.

The first thing most florists suggest for the home wedding is incorporating

A sophisticated topiary of fresh flowers needs little floor space (below left). A wedding wreath hangs from a mirror (below center), its gardenias perfuming the air for passersby. Every season provides bounty for gatepost and lamppost; matching ribbons flutter gaily (below right).

regional flowers or plants into the arrangements. Gerald Palumbo of Seasons Floral
Design Studio in New York City, suggests
taking flowers, greens, branches, and herbs
from the family's garden or its environs for

A flower girl's cluster of fat white daisies
(above left) connotes innocence and
magic. There can never be too many
flowers at a wedding; even a good-natured
pet might join in with a hefty garland of
blossoms (above right).

centerpieces and bouquets—"just be sure not to leave the garden bare." A
Georgia wedding might mix peach blossoms with grasses from local fields, a
Midwest farm wedding might incorporate sunflowers from the backyard.

 If regional blooms don't thrill you or simply don't match your wedding scheme, consider other varieties available from local florists or those in
more exotic locales. Little trees and large plants can be rented from nurseries
for more foliage.

Arranged flowers aren't the only choice. The popularity of home weddings is reflective of our love of gardens, and they can make a spectacular backdrop to a marriage celebration. If time and motivation allow, do extra plantings a year in advance. A florist can always add potted plantings if the results are not the right color or abundant enough.

Centerpieces vary as much as fingerprints, their size and shape often determined by the tables you're using. Cabaret tables with unassigned seating call for small centerpieces that can withstand a lot of activity. For example, a single stout pillar candle wrapped in a twist of vine, a potted plant, or a rose bowl won't be bothered by the comings and goings of dancing and second helpings. Long banquet tables also demand smaller centerpieces so they don't obscure the view from one end to the other. A graceful meandering trail of flowers along the length of the tabletop is a beautiful treatment. With larger round tables, play with high and low arrangements, wrought-iron stands, galvanized buckets, and topiary sculptures.

A gardening enthusiast chose a potted plant to create a focal point—and party favors—for a reception (below left). Freshly cut flowers casually placed in a large glass bowl have a whimsical effect (below right). Opposite: Professional arrangements (top left, center left, and bottom left) look soigné and very formal. Centerpieces don't have to be uniform from table to table; in two arrangements (top right and bottom right), different containers were used to dictate the colors of the arrangements.

Where Vows Are Taken

FINDING THE RIGHT PLACE for the ceremony is a mix of the practical and the aesthetic. First the practical: Is there enough room to create an altar or chuppah? Is there space for the participants in the ceremony to stand comfortably? Is there an area in front to accommodate all invited guests (whether standing or seated) and to create an aisle? Is the view unobstructed for most guests? If it's an outdoor location, will it be safe from wind, rain, flooding, wilting sun, and other whims of nature? Will it be private and quiet enough?

Next come the aesthetic considerations. If the wedding is indoors, look at the views from windows and at architectural features, such as bays and alcoves, to frame the ceremony. For outdoor weddings, the backdrop can be a beautiful view of a lake, the ocean, or a field. A hedge, an effusion of hydrangeas, a grove of trees, or a fountain can also serve as an anchor for the site. Try to find a natural niche, such as a pond or an intersection of stone walls. If there is no such space, create one with an archway woven with grapevines. Two large urns filled with flowers or a cluster of fat cylindrical candles flanking the couple work beautifully as well.

Fabric and candles lend a sense of volume and movement to a ceremonial site. A swath of linen or tulle hanging from the boughs of a tree, softly undulating in the breeze, is ethereal; flames that flicker lightly in wrought-iron candlesticks are magical. One designer placed candles in glass cylinders and hung them at different heights in a tree behind the altar for an evening wedding. Preserve jars used in the same manner blend with a rural setting. Lanterns placed on top of wooden posts are another modern way to evoke the feeling of a sacred fire.

Clockwise from top left: A ceremony in a small courtyard is private and romantic. With a beautiful view as a background, a runner of loose flower blossoms is enough to lead the eye. An arbor densely packed with flowers stands in perfect contrast to the wild waterfront property. A chuppah fashioned from a trellis boasts an effusion of blooms around each pole. A simple arched pergola of flowering branches shelters a pew. An alcove of shrubbery acts as a mini temple, complete with a raised platform, carpet, and curtain of loose cloth that waves in the breeze.

A Warm Welcome

GREETING GUESTS STARTS before they arrive—especially for those coming from out of town. Small booklets and programs reiterating directions and the day's schedule, left in snack baskets at their hotel, are a welcome courtesy. Some brides distribute friends' cell phone numbers so lost souls can call for last-minute directions. (Just be sure to have all phones turned off before the wedding march begins!)

A few markers in the immediate vicinity of the ceremony and reception are always helpful. They should be a seamless part of the wedding's overall style. Bright orange balloons, though cheerful, visible, and helpful, would seem out of sync with an all-white aesthetic. Simple bouquets of Fabric, such as the swag of tulle festooning a WELCOME sign (opposite), can be used along with flowers to identify the wedding house. A tasteful request that guests turn off pagers and cell phones appears in an elegant silver frame at the entrance to a ceremony (below left). A sign pointing to the reception site was professionally lettered (below center). An easy-to-spot sign, adorned with a bouquet mimicking the bride's, directs the way to the parking area (below right).

flowers, drapes of cloth, or smaller, more discreet signs would be a better choice. If the wedding is taking place in an apartment building, place markers out front, in the lobby, on the elevator, in the hallway, and at the apartment door. These markers not only make the day easier on guests, but also ease the pressure on the person in charge of keeping things running smoothly. A ceremony that is scheduled to take an hour and a half can be dragged out to almost twice that if guests stray. It's a good idea to indicate where to go every step of the way to keep people moving. For example, if the parking is

at the school down the street, the ceremony in the backyard, a receiving line and cocktail reception in the front yard, and the guest book in the house, guests may get stuck socializing at any of these points along the way, or might miss one altogether.

Of course, these signs don't literally have to be posted with words at each point. A path can be marked with potted plants, votive candles, or hurricane lamps. It's even a good idea to indicate the way to bathrooms or baby rooms, the bar, and food stations. When all else fails, have someone present who will keep an eye out for wayward guests and graciously hustle them along.

A literal sign pointing to the wedding is often unnecessary. For a ranch wedding, an ingenious couple lined the long driveway with photos of themselves as children (above). At a more formal affair, drapes of white gossamer cloth graced the drive leading to the wedding site, adding an artistic note (opposite).

A Quiet Little Corner

WEDDINGS SEEM TO HAPPEN IN WAVES, and although yours, of course, will stand out above the rest, your guests may have attended five others in the last couple of months—especially in the spring or summer. They may have gone out of their way to attend, devoting a fair amount of time and effort and incurring travel expenses. Some may begin to feel like perpetual prisoners of the nuptial scene. So it's important to make your wedding as much a highlight for them as it is for you. Show them how important they are to you. Besides your welcome waiting for them in their hotel rooms, courtesies you can offer them at home as well go a long way toward making people feel appreciated. Leave amenities baskets in the bathrooms and in any other room you're making available to your guests; embellish the baskets with flowers and fill them

with aspirin, antacid, sewing kits, hairpins, clear nail polish, spray deodorant, safety pins, pantyhose, Band-Aids, toothpaste, dental floss, and so on. Create a vanity area just outside outdoor toilets with a small table and chairs, and hang a mirror on the side.

One of the wonderful advantages of a home wedding is that people can roam around and relax more. Make sure it's clear that they are welcome to do so by placing tables and chairs throughout the house or on the property. Some

A quiet table by the swimming pool offers a cool retreat for guests or bride and groom (opposite left). An elaborate rest area with a divan, chairs, and pillows lets guests repose in style (opposite right). An informal, garden cocktail lounge (above) offers wicker chairs and tables, and a tent or two for those who want to get out of the sun.

brides ask friends to show guests around. Others put out photo albums, books, magazines, and even games for young ones to enjoy. Outfit a room for children with toys and a baby-sitter or two—this will surely feel like a gift from heaven to harried parents. Make sure to put tables and chairs in quiet, shaded locations where older guests can sit and rest. These quiet little corners don't need to be decorated extensively; a few candles, a shallow bowl of water with floating flowers on a coffee table, or a pretty lantern may be all that's necessary. Opening these additional spaces to guests will also allow for a more fluid, social atmosphere; they may mingle more if they don't feel restricted to their table and the dance floor.

A single table and chairs provide an intimate setting for a brief pause (above left). Guests take advantage of a hammock in the shade for a quiet chat (above right). Offering a room where guests can freshen up is a hospitable gesture. A simple sign lets them know where they are welcome (opposite).

Sentimental Journeys

PLANES, TRAINS, AND AUTOMOBILES, golf carts, boats, and flatbeds—just about every mode of transportation imaginable has been used to convey the bride, groom, and their guests from parking place to ceremony, to reception and home.

Special transportation is often necessary for a home wedding. Sufficient parking is not usually available right near the home, the walkway

may be rough (if it exists at all), and on large properties, there might be hundreds of yards between the ceremony and the reception tent. Though some guests may enjoy the walk, others might dread the trek. A friend of the groom in a carriage or a cart will seem like a knight in shining armor to a woman in high heels facing a field to cross. Some couples hire drivers to ensure revelers' highway safety.

Transportation is not only essential —it is the logistical detail couples have the most fun with. On one end of the spectrum, it presents an opportunity to indulge in fantasy. At what other time will you

The lap of luxury: A bride exits an elegant limousine (above left). Leased school buses (above right) can convey guests to and from a central parking area and help the day run smoothly. One wedding party makes the most of a cottage setting by approaching the ceremony in a speedboat (opposite).

have the chance to experience the magic of a horse-drawn carriage, the romance of a vintage automobile, the Arthurian dream of a white stallion, or the thrill of a racy speedboat, wedding gown and all? Being adventurous with transportation is a great way to inject energy and humor into a generally formal occasion. It's an icebreaker for guests as well; whether thrown together in a camel procession or on a school bus, they're likely to share a laugh or two.

On the other hand, the mode you choose could simply be another way to communicate a part of who you are and where you are from. For one Texas wedding, the bride and her father rode to the ceremony in a wagon pulled by the horses he had raised; another bride made her appearance on horseback. Whatever you do, remember: This is your wedding. Announce it.

Another chance to get creative: the getaway car in tune with the wedding's scheme. One couple rented a trolley car (above left). An urban twosome hailed a cab, then threw on some quick decorations (above right).

HOUSE-READY *Checklist*

PEOPLE OPT FOR church weddings and hotel receptions precisely to avoid taking on the level of organization involved in such an event. Those facilities are already equipped for the traffic of four hundred shoes, the trash of two hundred hungry eaters, the electrical demands of the band, the baker, and the salad maker; their toilets can handle 1,001 flushes. But don't despair—a little organization can go a long way.

❖ Have an electrician make sure your house has the electrical capacity to handle coffee urns, amps, portable johns, and extensive lighting—all it takes is one appliance too many and your guests will be eating in the dark. If there isn't enough power, the electrician can increase your supply permanently at relatively little expense. If the event is more than a hundred yards from the house, you'll need to rent generators.

❖ Check outlets. Two-pronged electrical outlets in many old homes will not accept today's three-pronged appliances. Arm yourself with converters (or ask your caterer to do so).

❖ Make sure you have extension cords; check that they're long enough and that they're in working condition.

❖ For an evening wedding, test the lighting two days before the event, and again the night before to make sure it creates the desired effect.

❖ Have enough fire extinguishers. Your local fire department can give you the necessary guidelines.

❖ Make arrangements for garbage disposal. Think ahead in terms of recycling bottles and cans.

❖ If you're relying on your own bathrooms, pump out the septic system. A backup can be an unpleasant surprise that's impossible to ignore.

❖ Water the lawn for the last time three days before the party so the grass isn't wet. Don't mow it for a few days; longer grass is hardier.

KEEP IN MIND the following chores, to be taken care of no more than a day or two before the wedding:

❖ Outfit the bathrooms with a generous supply of toilet tissue, guest towels, and soap.

❖ Fill the cars with gas.

❖ Buy extra bug spray, candles, hurricane lamps, and batteries.

❖ Wipe down the tables and chairs.

Magical Music

MUSIC IS A POWERFUL tool for affecting the mood and tempo of a gathering. A musical interlude between the ceremony and the reception can move the tone from solemnity to merriment. It is for this reason that a different kind of music is often used at every stage of a wedding, from the prelude before the ceremony to the processional and recessional, to party melodies and dance tunes. A Texas couple hired a mariachi band to play during the receiving line and a swing band for the reception.

However, hiring several different bands might not work for every budget. Keep in mind that the fewer the players the lower the cost, so a flutist or

harpist will cost less than a string quartet, a disc jockey less than a band. One bride cut corners by hooking up huge speakers and a fine stereo system a hundred yards from her house, then blasting her favorite Beethoven under the sky's blue dome. Another asked her friends to play their own instruments during the ceremony.

The songs played on a couple's wedding day will forever be music to their ears, whether from a band with a calypso beat (above left) or a simple guitar trio (above right). Opposite, clockwise from top: A classical quartet and vocalist perform during the ceremony; a bagpipe player acts as the pied piper to the reception; a jazz band picks up the pace of a tent party.

You may not want a four-piece rock band with amps blowing the roof off. Choose the music, and number of players, appropriate to the size of the room. Place them out of the way of foot traffic, the caterer, and the exits.

The Importance of Lighting

WHETHER THE DESIRED EFFECT is that of a romantic dining area or a raging dance floor, lighting plays a huge role in any wedding. "Lighting is really key in a tent or a home," says party planner Elizabeth Allen. "It's something that many people overlook. You've hired a florist. You've bought a beautiful dress. You've decorated the place. But if the surroundings and the flowers and you aren't properly lit, it falls flat." Lighting can enhance or destroy an environment, make faces look rosy and sexy or tired and old, highlight decorations or overpower them. When used artfully, it can create an unforgettable air of drama.

Consultants can work wonders with theatrical and landscape lighting, both inside a tent or house and outside. White tents are the perfect canvas on which to play with patterns and colors of bulbs and gels. Pink and white tones can provide enough light so the photographer won't need a flash. Soft blue tones lend themselves to a more formal evening atmosphere. Pinspot lights aimed at each tabletop, with spaces of darkness between them, allow for a sense of privacy conducive to conversation, as do smaller clusters of subdued lighting away from the dining area.

Use lighting to make the most of a space, not to transform it. Inside the home, embellish and highlight architectural details that add character to the room, such as friezes and molding. Highlight the rustic beams in a barn; uplight trees and gardens.

Professional theatrical lighting can add at least five thousand dollars to your budget. If you're going the do-it-yourself route, experiment early on with gels, lamps, and landscape bulbs, available at home supply stores. Some rules of thumb: Rosy and amber tones are generally the most flattering. Light up, not down, to avoid glare. If your efforts result in a tent lit like a gym, add more gels to soften them. Put lanterns into the mix. And don't forget the power of candles.

Lights are fantastically dramatic and one of the most economical ways to add to a wedding's visual impact. For this one night only, the impractical and the seemingly impossible should be considered—even a wreath of slow-burning candles above the front door (opposite). The final addition: Garlands of bee lights wind their way up porch columns toward the candles.

Food and Menu Planning

THOUGH A HOME WEDDING may be a catered affair, you can still put your stamp on it. Work with your caterer to create a menu that reflects your tastes—literally—and personal style. Even a simple reception with tea and tiny madeleines makes a statement. Choose regional ingredients. Use a family recipe. Present your favorite food. Make it yours.

Keep in mind the tone you want to set, your budget, the time of the celebration, and the complexion of the guest list. If possible, take note of food allergies, vegetarians, and fickle eaters or kids who would be delighted with a hamburger. Be generous with the Chamapagne and wine—this is, after all, a very important celebration—but be sure to have plenty of non-alcoholic beverages on hand as well.

The menu you select will dictate the tone and formality of your meal more than how you present it; remember, no matter what kind of china and silverware you use, barbecue is barbecue, and it's always informal. At a home wedding, just about any choice goes, from standing cocktails with finger foods before dancing to an elaborate multicourse sit-down dinner complete with wait staff. Bistro-style service is an elegant, moderately formal option.

If you're hiring a caterer, ask if their price per person is for food and beverage only, or for food plus service and rental equipment. (Service and rental can actually double the cost.) Substitutions in your menu will help keep you within your budget. If your heart is set on serving beef tenderloin and cost is an issue, offer it as an hors d'oeuvre, sliced thinly on toast points, instead of as a main course. If you want an informal wedding that still smacks of indulgence but can't afford oysters on the half shell and a whole lobster for each guest, serve lobster bisque with breaded haddock.

A final note: Make sure to offer hors d'oeuvres to guests the minute they arrive at the party. Food really gets things going.

Clockwise from top left: A server passes food at a tented reception. Menu cards let guests know what to expect— and they're great souvenirs. Guests can help themselves to a simple yet elegant repast of iced tea, lemonade, miniature sandwiches, and strawberries and cream. A contemporary finger food favorite: easy-to-eat sushi. Champagne is poured out just before guests arrive.

Wedding Cakes

TRADITIONALLY, THE WEDDING CAKE, symbolic of the bride, was white, delicate, and pristine in shape—one didn't see many sand castle or sailboat wedding cakes, or even simple carrot cakes. A second cake, the groom's cake, usually chocolate, was also offered. Since the 1970s, wedding cakes have been liberated. Flavors, decorations, and shapes of every description have become commonplace. Even so-called traditional cakes sport

freshly cut flowers, colorful details, or different flavors for each tier. One bride chose decorations that echoed the lace on her gown. For a gazebo wedding, a replica of the structure was made from icing for the cake top. Still another couple chose edible flowers that complemented the

Though the icing is typically white, the decorative touches on a cake are often colorful; flowers can be real (and pesticide-free) or iced. A three-tier white cake is accented with creamy roses (opposite), while pale hydrangeas decorate another confection (above left). Icing flowers in vibrant colors offer a tempting treat for the guests at a wedding picnic (above right).

bridal bouquets. But if just about anything goes, there are still some limits to the size of the cake and the kind of icing that will work: Rolled fondant, for example, is best for more intricate icing; it is sturdier than buttercream.

Cake experts stress that couples living in a relatively populated area who plan to marry in the spring should reserve a cake at least six months ahead, a year if possible. Some brides wait until they've chosen their gowns or other details so they can match the cake to them. But you can still reserve in advance since the color and flavor aren't finalized until right before the party. Bakers stress the importance of a sturdy cake table on a solid surface to avoid collapses, and of using the right frosting for your climate. They know from experience what it takes for a three-tier cake to gradually slide into a heap on its side.

A couple expressed their sense of humor by topping their cake with a laminated photograph of themselves in wedding attire (above left). A more traditional version depicts perfect romantic love (above right). Wedding cakes aren't always visions in white; a multitiered selection of small cupcakes (opposite) makes a welcome change for the eyes and tastebuds.

You Were Never Lovelier

THE VISION OF A BRIDE walking down the aisle is always unforgettable. She looks confident, unique, utterly beautiful. Her attire, whether traditional gown and veil, family heirloom, or cutting-edge designer creation, symbolizes one of the most important events of her life. Because she may have envisioned herself as a bride since she was little, the choice of her dress is a very emotional decision. But emotion is one thing; stress is another. Nothing should keep her from relishing every detail, from buying the gown to choosing the accessories to dressing on the day of the wedding. ✤

Dressed to Thrill

"A WEDDING GOWN is like no other purchase," says Michelle Roth of Michelle Roth & Co. in New York City. Henry Weinreich, her brother and partner, agrees: "Not only does it represent one of the most important days of your life, it actually plays a huge role in what other people in the wedding party wear, and in shaping the feel of the entire day."

The significance of that purchase weighs heavily on some brides. But shopping for your wedding dress is an event that should be enjoyed; after all, this is an excuse to buy the most exquisite piece of clothing you've ever laid eyes on. To make it easier, leave as much time as possible for your search. Have a notion of what the perfect dress should be before investing hours in trying on several hundred, and seek the help of one or two trusted advisers rather than a gaggle of minions. Look through magazines, check out designers' Web sites, study catalogs from bridal boutiques. Don't try to change your whole look for your wedding day—consider dresses that look like *you*. And don't buy a dress just because you love the buttons, the sleeves, or the way it drapes through the waist. Love the whole dress, not its details. If you can picture yourself walking down the aisle in it, chances are you've found the right one. "When a bride realizes this is the dress, a lightness comes over her face. Then, some laugh, some cry, some look relieved," says Roth.

The kind of event you're planning will certainly play a role in your choice of dress. Tulle, organza and crepe, for example, work beautifully for outdoor weddings. Heavier fabrics like silk satins suit more formal, indoor events. Home weddings, generally less formal than church weddings, may involve a shorter aisle and traipsing through grass, so a bride might want to think before getting an ultra-formal wedding gown complete with crinoline, petticoats, a long train, and a cathedral veil.

Not all women dream of wearing a wedding gown, especially those marrying later on in life. For the past hundred years,

Clockwise, from top left: Exquisite lace embellishes a classic gown with long sleeves and a high neckline. A fitted silk-satin bodice with a full tulle skirt is the epitome of romance. A sleek and modern version of the bridal gown is complete with illusion back and sleeves and oversize cuffs. Proper stuffing ensures a sleeveless dress will look crisp when the bride walks down the aisle.

brides have traditionally worn floor-length gowns of white—from candle white to ivory to taupe—embellished with lace, pearls, embroidery, or flowers, and accessorized with trains and veils. (We have Queen Victoria to thank for that; before her marriage in 1840, brides wore all manner of color and adornment.) Today, as brides become increasingly independent and modern, the styles they choose are equally varied and contemporary. Color is enjoying a renaissance—everything from icy blue silks to vibrant ruby satins—and more and more brides are opting for narrower silhouettes in slinkier fabrics, with low backs and plunging necklines. Those who don't want the conventional look can go with something very tailored, such as a formal suit in off-white silk, or a beaded cashmere sweater set with a taffeta or satin ball-gown skirt. Shrugs, stoles, boleros, capes, and little mohair jackets in shades of white are an elegant way to top off any dress or gown for a winter or nighttime wedding. Many brides take advantage of the day by wearing a dress by the designer of their dreams. "The essential thing is to take the tradition and make it relevant," says Roth. "A bride can easily find elements of traditional bridal attire in a more modern design."

Weinreich advises brides to treat their gown like a person ("If it's hot out, put it in a room with air conditioning") and to keep it in a place free of pets, prying eyes, and sticky fingers. Remove the outer plastic but keep the form or stuffing in the dress, and hang it on a hook five inches from the wall so it won't get flattened. If it has a train, remove it from the hanger and let it fall to the ground. (Make sure the floor is covered with a sheet.) Store lingerie in a drawer with dry cotton wool that's been steeped in perfume; by the day of your wedding, a simple sigh or the shrug of your shoulders will release a gentle hint of fragrance.

New York hair and makeup artist Nelson D' Leon suggests finding the right hairstyle for your face—and your gown—before buying any accessories. His best-tested advice to brides-to-be: Cut a white T-shirt to match the neckline of your dress and wear it when you have your hair done, then go shopping for your headpiece, veil, and jewelry.

For an indoor home wedding, a not-quite-so-formal gown that won't overwhelm a small space might be appropriate. This imported silk damask dress with princess lines—a vision of utter simplicity—is a good choice for all four seasons as well.

The veil should work with the proportions of your height, the shape of your dress, and the formality of your wedding. A fingertip length is appropriate for most women and long enough to be very glamorous. Shorter veils, such as the blusher and the flyaway, work well for brides with a playful sensibility. The longest are harder to wear and maneuver, but they are incredibly dramatic. Examples of longer versions are the ballerina, which comes to just above the ankles; the sweep, which brushes the floor; the chapel, which pools slightly on the floor; and the cathedral, which trails like a train. They are quite formal and may seem out of place in the middle of a bucolic field, but if it's your dream to wear one, you can make it work.

Now consider headpieces. If it's not your style to wear much jewelry, you may decide to forgo a headpiece altogether. If you do decide on one, gown, hairstyle, and veil are the determining factors. On one end of the spectrum are tiaras, if it is the fairy-tale princess look you're hoping to achieve. They look best with upswept hair. On the other end are single flowers, wreaths, headbands, combs, and barrettes. In between are garlands of silk flowers, tailored hats, or sun hats. All can be worn unadorned, or encrusted with gold, silver, or real or

A wedding is the perfect occasion to splurge on beautiful lingerie and shoes (below left). Shoes and hats for the bride and her attendants should be stored in labeled boxes to keep them dust-free (below right).

costume jewels. Be sure whatever you choose is securely fastened to both the veil and your hair; people will be hugging you for hours.

Before buying a veil, practice in it: Turn in it. Walk around in it. If it makes you shiver every time it brushes your back, don't buy it. "The right veil brings out a certain feeling," says Roth. "It's magical. It's a shame to take it off for the party."

Jewelry, too, depends on how elaborate the rest of your ensemble will be. "Don't buy everything at once," D' Leon advises. "Go slowly. That way, any impulse buys will only involve one mistake instead of many." A complete set of matching accessories can make a woman look like someone else's idea of a bride; and every special bangle and bauble in the family may well be too much. Accessories should be simple, especially if there is any beadwork on the gown or veil. Don't wear dangling earrings with a headpiece and an embroidered bodice. If there are flowers on the neckline of the dress, a simple pair of diamond or pearl studs may be all you need.

Accessories are a wonderful way to turn up the glamour. A fingertip veil embellished with flowers (above left) always looks lovely. A crystal tiara and drop earrings can add an aristocratic touch (above center). A feather stole and hat offer warmth and drama for a winter wedding (above right).

Bridal Bouquets

"NOSEGAYS—SMALL, UNDERSTATED clusters of mostly bright flowers—are perfect for a home wedding," says Preston Bailey of Preston Bailey Entertainment and Set Design in New York City. "A bouquet of one kind of flower is always lovely, too, whether you choose roses or stephanotis." An effusion of white lilacs conveys a fresh spring look; a gathering of sweet

peas has a straight-from-the-garden appeal. Collages of pale, delicate blossoms are always popular; today there is a trend toward bold colors as well—one New York bride carried a heavy bouquet of black magic roses at her October wedding.

Bailey suggests that all flowers sit in water for as long as possible before being made into a bouquet for maximum staying power. He also recommends gathering stems in a French twist and wrapping them in ribbon to avoid water stains.

A lily of the valley bouquet is the classic, appropriate for any wedding (above left). A wedding bouquet can incorporate more than one flower: A diverse collection of blooms adds a vivid note to the proceedings (above center). White calla lilies, secured with a white ribbon (above right), make a sophisticated statement. Sweet peas, tulips, and roses are always sublime (opposite).

Dressing Up

IT SEEMS ONLY FITTING that the women closest to you be present for the beauty ritual preceding the celebration. It should be reminiscent of the slumber parties, beauty days, and pre–"night out on the town" preenings you may have spent together as girlfriends, sisters, or mother and daughter. If possible, arrange to have hair and makeup done at home. This will reduce stress and hassle. It will seem like there is a lot going on when you are surrounded by the buzz and flitters of the hairdresser and makeup stylist, your mother and female relatives, the wedding party, and any other fairy godmother types present, but try to keep the pace relaxed. The atmosphere should be calming, nurturing, and feminine. Take deep breaths, eat something light, drink plenty of water, and pace yourself.

Start your day with a walk or other exercise to expend nervous energy, then shower with a soap or gel that matches your fragrance. Apply hand and body lotion in the same scent before you put on perfume. Fragrance layering will ensure that the scent lasts and you won't have to worry about heavy doses of strong perfume. If you're having a massage, make sure the oils used will either wash off or won't clash with these other products.

Getting into a wedding dress should be a little ceremony of its own. One of the women present should be dressed already to help you into your gown and headpiece. Have on hand an emergency kit when you're dressing: three pairs of pantyhose, extra earring backs, safety pins, hairpins, straight pins, pretty slippers, shoes (which have been broken in), a sewing kit, and any medicines you may need, including smelling salts, papaya enzyme or antacid tablets for a nervous stomach, aspirin and decongestants for allergies.

Most of all, says wedding dress designer Anthony Muto, a bride should "savor every moment of getting into that dress. This is one time when she shouldn't be doing anything just for convenience."

A bride's closest friends and relatives are on hand to help prepare, pitching in wherever needed—adjusting the veil, fixing a sandal strap, fastening hard-to-reach buttons, or polishing the hairstyle. There's always someone around to help the flower girls as well.

HAIR AND BEAUTY *Checklist*

THE EFFECT YOU WANT to achieve with your beauty regime and makeup the day of the wedding is to look like yourself, but a little bit more glamorous. If you like a clean and natural look, stay with clean and natural makeup. If you're someone who owns only one tube of lipstick, use that tube. Contrary to popular opinion, says Kaija Berzins Braus, a wedding photographer in New York City, heavy makeup is not necessary for good wedding photographs. What is necessary is that the bride look and feel like herself.

- Use Nelson D' Leon's trick of wearing a T-shirt that has been cut to duplicate the neckline of your gown to hair and makeup consultations.

- Have a custom-blended foundation made that matches the color of the skin on your chest. Bring it with you if you're having a professional do your makeup.

- Have your hair trimmed and colored, if necessary, at least a week in advance.

- If you wax or pluck any facial hair, do so at least two days before so your skin won't look irritated.

- Have a massage, manicure, and pedicure the day before. Neutral polishes are generally recommended. If you want more flair, choose a pearl finish.

- Before applying foundation, apply your own moisturizer to a base that will hold your makeup through the day. An oil-free one will keep you from getting shiny.

- Pay more attention than usual to eye makeup and eyebrow grooming.

- Single false eyelashes add glamour and drama in a subtle way.

- In the event of an impending blemish and no time to see a dermatologist, apply a generous dollop of cortisone cream on the spot, cover it with a Band-Aid, and sleep on it. Toothpaste applied directly on a blemish will help speed up the drying process, and eyedrops will literally get the red out of one.

- Get a facial at least four days before the wedding. Resist the temptation to have a kind of facial you haven't had before or to try any new skin-care products or makeup right before—you never know how your skin will respond.

- Similarly, this is not the time to experiment with a new hairstyle; you may poke at and fidget with those tresses all evening, or feel self-conscious in a new 'do.

- Remember that the hairdo you wear for the ceremony is the hairdo you'll wear for hours greeting, hugging, eating, and dancing. Can it withstand the excitement?

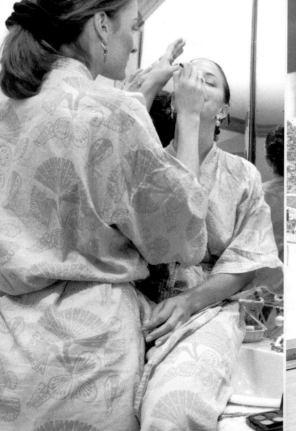

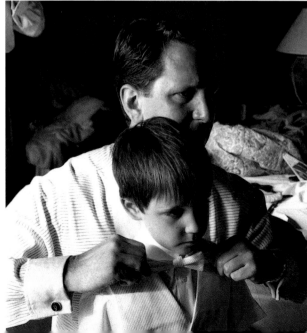

The Fashionable Man

THERE MAY SEEM TO BE FEWER wardrobe details with which men need to be concerned, but don't be fooled—traditionally they follow as strict a dress code as their fiancées when shopping for their wedding attire. Formal nuptials call for a dark gray or black cutaway tuxedo with a gray vest, gray striped trousers, and a wing-collar shirt. A less formal outfit would be a single-breasted gray or black stroller (a coat with a rounded tail) and trousers. Moderately dressy, and appropriate for most occasions, is a dark-colored suit.

As with the bride at a home wedding, the rules tend to be flexible or nonexistent. A navy blue blazer and off-white pants could be just the ticket for an afternoon seaside or waterfront wedding. A ranch-style party might

call for crisp black Wranglers, a cowboy hat, and boots. An evening reception in a townhouse might be formal enough for strollers or cutaways and striped trousers. Groomsmen generally dress almost identically to the groom.

With so much attention paid to the bride and her attendants, it could be easy to forget about the groom and his men. Make space for them, too, and don't leave them to fend for themselves. A friend or relative can help with the trickier parts of getting ready.

Within the confines of tradition, the groom can express his personal style with a colorful vest, necktie, or bow tie (the choice of which says a lot on its own), or witty cufflinks. He may even choose to forsake all convention. Whatever he wears, it should be something he is comfortable and confident in. And above all, if budget is an issue, "A good suit," says one wedding consultant, "is always better than a cheap tuxedo."

Gifts of Appreciation

THE GIFTS YOU GIVE the members of your wedding party serve as tokens of appreciation and friendship. The best time to present them is at the rehearsal dinner the night before, during the bridesmaids' luncheon the day of the wedding, or right before the ceremony—if time allows. They don't need to be extravagant, but they should be meaningful, a symbol of your friendship as well as a memento of the day. Engraving, etching, or monogramming their names or initials and the day of the wedding is one way to personalize any gift.

While the bride and groom can select a unique gift for each attendant, different versions of the same gift can create a sense of unity—for the bridesmaids beaded handbags in different colors, for each groomsman cufflinks reflecting his favorite sport or hobby. If you're going to select matching gifts, women will appreciate silk scarves, keepsake journals, crystal Champagne flutes. Wallets, pocket knives, and silver money clips make handsome gifts for the groomsmen. Gifts involving part of the wedding attire itself is especially thoughtful—jewelry for the women, neckties for the men.

Additional keepsake ideas for both men and women are embroidered linen hand towels in a favorite color, engraved silver pens, engraved silver flasks, crystal or silver water pitchers, or picture frames complete with photographs of your times together. Another thoughtful gift is to invest in a set of leatherbound antique books of classics and poetry, choosing one for each attendant and inscribing it with a short note of appreciation.

Tasteful souvenirs for your guests are always a thoughtful, and much appreciated, gesture. Such gifts can be smaller versions of those for your attendants—consider miniature picture frames in the same style as the larger ones you presented to your bridal party, for example. Guests' party favors might also echo the theme of the wedding itself, such as a small pot of flowers or herbs for a garden party. Placing one at each table setting or at the door will provide guests with something to remember your day, long after the party's over.

Thoughtful gifts for attendants and guests show your appreciation for all their help and patience (opposite left and right). Pretty blooms in terra-cotta pots do double duty as table decorations and party favors (above left). Young saplings dressed in burlap and ribbon are the perfect souvenir for an informal wedding by a lake (above right).

Capturing the Memories

WEDDINGS FLY BY. It is as important to stop throughout the day to take mental snapshots as it is to have someone there to document it for you, lest the excitement leave you with nothing but a blur. "I love showing brides photographs of their weddings because so often they've forgotten everything," says New York photographer Kaija Berzins Braus. "Sometimes

when I give them the photos, it almost feels like I'm giving them the gift of their memories. When they see the pictures, the day comes back to them."

If you're hiring a professional photographer, be very specific about what you want, and schedule his or her time accordingly. Do you want individual portraits of family and the wedding party? Do you prefer a series of candid photographs throughout the day? Would you like a photographic record of all the preparations leading up to the big event? If you hire both a videographer and a still photographer, make sure they can work together. Otherwise, you

Say cheese! A shot of a large group of guests (above left) captures the mood of the party. A bride and her flower girls (above right) look relaxed in an informal portrait. Opposite, clockwise from top left: A touching image captures the most important members of the day. A young wedding participant shows her excitement. A bride poses in full regalia. The bride and groom steal a romantic moment.

may see the videographer in the background of every photograph, and the photographer in every frame of the video!

Always ask for references, and try to arrange a face-to-face meeting with each candidate. The personality of the photographer may be just as important in your decision as the quality of the photography. Do you want someone who seems invisible, or do you want someone getting people to pose and smile? The choice depends on your own personal style; just make sure it matches the photographer's way of working—and that he or she makes you want to smile.

Keep in mind that portrait photography requires a lot of time. Be sure to schedule your day so much of it can be completed before the ceremony—

that way it won't interfere with the natural course of the reception and party. "You should be spending this precious time with friends and family who've traveled from all over, not with a photographer," remarks Berzins Braus.

No matter how beautiful the professional photography, the spontaneous snapshots taken by friends often seem to be the most fun. Encourage the amateur photographer in each of them by handing out disposable cameras, or by having a "picture potluck" basket at the exit, in which guests can leave a mystery roll of their own film when they leave.

Parents of the groom pose in their finest for an informal portrait (opposite). Studio-quality portraits can be taken at home, as three photos by Keith Trumbo attest (above).

FOUR HOURS
and Counting

THE BIG DAY ARRIVES, but much remains to be done. Sharing the duties of pre-ceremony preparations is an opportunity for the bride and groom to ease their parents' worries and to show trust in their friends by delegating tasks. It also allows friends to show how much they care by happily seeing to last-minute arrangements, by lending a hand to older guests, by helping the bride and groom laugh off the jitters. Because these people are part of the couple's closest circle, just the chance to band together as dear friends is reason—and thanks—enough. ❖

With Help from Friends

DON'T SHY AWAY FROM making this a team effort. The more hands-on the experience is for loved ones, the more memorable and rewarding it will be. This is certainly so for do-it-yourself affairs, and may be encouraged by wedding planners and caterers as well.

Friends often go to great lengths to help out at a wedding. They complete tasks as heroic as building an emergency hurricane shelter to making a party of pitching and decorating a tent, complete with makeshift ottomans and a disco ball. But most of all, the time they spend with you in preparing for the event should be fun.

Some couples call their helpers the "house party" and officially acknowledge them in the program. This shows that they're part of your closest circle, even if they're not in the wedding party. Asking

Friends and family members can take care of many things, from assembling and decorating table numbers (below left), to arranging the floral decorations for the ceremony tent (below right), to emergency lifting and hauling (opposite).

for their help is one way to include friends you were unable to have as bridesmaids or ushers. Teenagers tend to be proud of such responsibilities and take them seriously. If your needs are extensive, you may want to host a luncheon for everyone involved well before the wedding and distribute a plan for the day; include the phone numbers of family members and each person in the wedding party.

On the day of the wedding, ask that this "support group" arrive early. Provide them with a room in which to store their attire and have a light meal ready for them (the preparations of which can also be the product of a friend's altruism), and enjoy their company.

DELEGATING *Checklist*

TRY TO ASSIGN TASKS to people with specific talents they can apply.

❖ Have a terrific organizer call to confirm every item on a comprehensive list of particulars: the arrival time of the rentals and/or tent; the arrangements for cake preparations; the schedules for caterers, bartenders, musicians, and clergy or officiant. Your taskmaster may even double-check wedding night accommodations and honeymoon reservations.

❖ Have someone draw up a time line of the day outlining the duties of the wedding party and readers, and distribute it. This person will also make sure that all involved are set, dressed, and ready to go at the time the ceremony is to begin.

❖ Have an artistic friend design the program, add final touches to decorations, and see to it that the amenities baskets are filled.

❖ Ask someone to fill the cars with gas, check on the propane tanks for the grill, and test the audio system.

❖ Ask your taller friends to put up the signs and balloons. Ask friends with young children to childproof the area and put fragile valuables away.

❖ A trusted diplomat can be charged with speaking with the caterer during the reception should anything go wrong. He

or she can also hand out the checks to various professionals at the end of the day.

❖ Appoint your most charming friends to watch over elderly guests or those with special needs, acting as helpmates and seeing to it that they aren't left alone. Ideally, there should be as many companions as there are people who may need them.

❖ Someone should be the keeper of the wedding guest book, making sure it (along with a pen) is where it should be and that people are signing it.

❖ It's not a bad idea to distribute "toast tips" to the attendants and family members who will be speaking at some point during the reception. Although they're likely to be brimming over with things to say about you, they may forget the simplest things, such as introducing themselves, in the heat of the moment. You might also want to remind them of any personal details you don't want raised!

❖ Name a friend to organize everyone for the bouquet toss—it can get a little hectic. This friend can also be the keeper of your gifts until you return from your honeymoon.

❖ Ask a tireless type to stay until the very end and oversee the donation of flowers and leftover food to charity.

CHECKLIST *for Participants*

DON'T ASSUME your bridal party knows what to do. If no rehearsal is planned, be sure all participants understand their roles.

❖ Bridesmaids and the maid of honor should arrive two hours early to help the bride dress. They all should be ready fifteen minutes before the ceremony.

❖ Ushers should be ready forty-five minutes before the ceremony. Their job is to escort female guests to their seats, and to oversee all seating for the service. They should be clearly instructed about how you want this done—who the key relatives are, and which ones might need special assistance. Traditionally, the bride's family sits on the left, the groom's on the right. The first two rows are reserved for the couples' immediate family, including grandparents; the next three are for extended family and closest friends.

❖ The ushers must make sure there are seats reserved for the readers and that they are accessible to the altar.

❖ The best man is in charge of making sure the ring or rings get to the ceremony.

❖ The maid of honor holds the bride's bouquet and attends to her needs (fixing her veil or train) during the ceremony.

❖ The flower girl should be ready with her basket of flower petals, the ring bearer with his pillow and ring.

❖ All participants—wedding party, readers, musicians—should be notified of the order and timing of the ceremony.

Setting Up

IDEALLY, THE PROCESS of setting up the reception tent or room happens over several days. Get as many details as possible out of the way ahead of the time. The tent should be pitched and the dance floor put down about three days in advance. House decorations and hardier floral arrangements can be done the day before to save last-minute rushing. Count all rentals, including tables, chairs, glassware, china, silverware, and linens, on their arrival.

Following a correct installation sequence allows the process to run smoothly. If the tent sides have been down and the weather permits, raise them to air out the tent during setup. Start outfitting the tent by decorating the tent poles and putting up lights. Take care of any electrical needs before tables are

A member of the catering staff adds the finishing touches to tables in a tent. Meticulous attention to detail and ample time to set up are essential.

brought in so that wires don't get tangled around table legs. Everything should be wiped down before setup; it takes only a day or two for items to collect a fine coat of dust or pollen, especially in an outdoor environment.

Creating a complete dining area is a team effort. Friends are each assigned one table to decorate (above left). The final assembly of the cake usually requires more than two hands as well (above right).

Service tables such as the buffets, the cake table, and the bar should be put in place before the dinner tables. Chairs should come last—to facilitate freedom of movement while setting up.

Next, lay the linens and put down the centerpieces, including candles and place cards. Tablecloths might need to be steamed first. Usually, passing hands firmly and vigorously over the cloth is sufficient to remove fold marks. And remember: If you're using air conditioning or heating, activate them during setup so that the environment is perfect when guests arrive.

Much of planning for a wedding and reception deals with minutiae, but after the linens are laid out, the places set, and the flowers arranged, take in the big picture. Step back. Look at the room as a whole. Are the arrangements at the same height? Are the tapers straight? Are all the chairs tucked in? Do the tables present a uniform appearance?

If you've hired a wedding planner or caterer, making sure that everything is in place is part of their responsibility, but keep certain things in mind when you give the room a final glance. When planning the party, you did an imaginary walk-through of the room to check the flow. Now is the time to test this for real. Is there enough room between tables for people to walk comfortably? Do the caterers have easy serving access? Make sure the cake is in a visible but safe and cool place. Remove any tools—scissors, ribbon, pins, and tape—used in the decorating process. Count chairs and settings again to make sure that each table is complete, and that place cards are in the correct place. Test the sound system.

With all of the above to consider, safety is a detail that sometimes goes unchecked. Electrical cords should be in a dry place and away from walkways so no one trips. If children will be present, cover electrical outlets and be sure that all fragile items are out of the reach of small hands. Be sure that candle flames will be nowhere near flower arrangements, ribbons, and napkins. Check that there aren't any wobbly table legs, that candlesticks are set squarely in their holders, and that the candles won't tip if the tables are jostled.

The final check (below left): Are chairs tucked in, plates centered? Is glassware sparkling, cake in place? Designate an area for gifts (below right).

ANYTHING THAT *Can Go Wrong...*

IN THE EVENT of a disaster, the most important thing is to stay calm and to maintain a sense of humor; as long as you do, other people will. In the real-life wedding pitfalls that follow, friends and family rose to the occasion, used their imagination, and kept the party going.

❖ A family hosting a backyard pre-reception party on the Maine coast was surprised by a drenching rain and a cold sea wind. In a matter of hours, they notified guests and moved the entire event, including food, flowers, and guests, to a friend's house.

❖ At a buffet reception, the caterer ran out of beef tenderloin, so some guests were offered vegetable plates for dinner. The hosts remained gracious and spoke to the caterer about it the next day.

❖ A Texas bride who had banked on flowers from her parents' property arrived home to find a drought. At the last minute, she chose more resilient flowers from the local florist.

❖ The floor of a backyard tent that was pitched over a swimming pool began creaking just as the guests were being seated. The tent was evacuated. Guests stood at its perimeter and watched in suspense as the ceremony proceeded—with just the wedding party present—on the unstable floor. The floor held.

❖ Days of rain before a horseback ceremony at the shore left the beach like quicksand, creating dangerous conditions—even though the weather had cleared by the day of the wedding. The family put a phone chain in motion, one person on the guest list calling another, until everyone was notified to go to the bride's home. Over coffee and doughnuts, all the wedding guests brainstormed for options, including a playground and football field. The group settled for a standing ceremony in front of a lighthouse. There was a loud cheer when the bride galloped up to the groom.

❖ One couple's Newport nuptials took place in what became a hurricane. Their tent company draped an extra layer of canvas over the tent, battened down the hatches, and pulled off the wedding without missing a beat.

❖ A three-tier wedding cake melted and sagged during the trip from the baker's to the bride's. The florist cut fresh flowers from the host's garden and created a new look that blended with the surroundings.

❖ Severe storms the day before a wedding caused the tent to collapse. The tent rental company couldn't (or wouldn't) send

someone out to repitch it, so the couple turned to their wedding designer for help. He sent the couple and their families to the movies, called another rental company, and had the tent back up before the families returned.

❖ After days of rain, the spot for the tent became totally flooded. The bride and her father ran to the hardware store for supplies and constructed a new floor for the tent. "They looked like they were having a great time," remembers their caterer.

One More Look in the Mirror

AT THIS STAGE, the most important thing for a pair of soon-to-be newlyweds to remember is to breathe deeply. Couples have various ways of dealing with butterflies. One bride said she did "face yoga"—puckering her lips, smiling broadly, opening her mouth and eyes wide, sticking out her tongue—to erase nervousness from her expression before walking down the aisle. If nothing else, these antics might provide a laugh, which is always a good way to lighten up.

Michelle Roth Bridal recommends that a bride take a few moments to move around in her dress, veil, and shoes. Make sure that the

Skirts are fluffed, buttons buttoned, veils pouffed, and slips straightened before the maid of honor, bridesmaids, flower girls, and, finally, the bride head for the aisle (below left). A well-behaved flower girl waits patiently as last-minute adjustments are made (below right).

headpiece doesn't slip with a turn of your head. If your shoes slip on the carpet, have a bridesmaid scuff them up

Mom helps tie the groom's bow (above left). Words of encouragement are given to the ring bearer (above right).

outside. This is your last chance to sew on a loose button or smooth a wisp of hair. But don't expect perfection; there will always be something that isn't exactly as planned. That said, apply a fresh coat of lipstick (and make sure there's none on your teeth), take a last sip of water, and breathe deeply again. If you want to sit down in your full attire, be careful not to crush your skirts or veil. A bridesmaid should spread them out around you. As you're walking out the door, the maid of honor should fluff the skirts and veil so that they fall smoothly.

The list might be shorter, but the groom and groomsmen have their own checklist: bow ties should be tied and neckties straightened, boutonnieres attached, jackets buttoned and shoes tied tightly. Sunglasses should be removed for the ceremony.

The Dream
COMES TRUE

THE CEREMONY—THE VOWS

you exchange, the music and readings you choose—

reflects your spirituality, your hopes and dreams, your

commitment to one another as a couple. You're sur-

rounded by all the people you love and who love you.

You look exquisite, and that remarkable person you've

just thrown your lot in with couldn't be happier. It's

time to stop worrying about every little detail and let

others take over so you can truly savor the biggest

party of your life. ❖

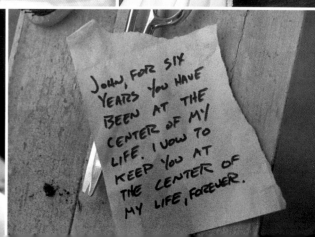

JOHN, FOR SIX
YEARS YOU HAVE
BEEN AT THE
CENTER OF MY
LIFE. I VOW TO
KEEP YOU AT
THE CENTER OF
MY LIFE, FOREVER.

A Warm Greeting

GUESTS SOMETIMES ARRIVE as much as forty-five minutes before a wedding begins, and often continue filing in until the last minute. Be sure your ushers or designated friends are ready, "on location," to greet them and direct them to their seats as they arrive.

Music playing in the background can create just the tone and atmosphere you want at this moment. Select tunes that will help set a quiet, reflective mood for the ceremony—anything from classical or jazz to vocal. Remember, you might need as much as an hour's worth of music.

This is a good time to have guests sign the wedding book. Once the party starts, this lovely tradition can get lost in the shuffle. Making the book available during these quiet moments will give guests time to write something more personal than just their names and addresses. And making programs available now will give them an idea of what to expect during the ceremony.

A young usher hands out programs as guests arrive for the ceremony (opposite). They'll be sure to sign a wedding book that sits invitingly on a table strewn with rose petals at the entrance (below left). A basket full of yarmulkes and wedding programs takes the place of an usher (below right).

The Ceremony

ONE OF THE ADVANTAGES of a home wedding is that, because yours is not one of several weddings booked in a public location that day, and because you don't have to abide by the conventions of church or temple, the timing can be more relaxed and the ceremony styled to your spiritual and personal preferences.

Weddings, whether religious or civil, tend to follow a similar sequence. Typical elements include a prelude, processional, opening remarks, songs,

readings, vows, exchange of rings or unity ritual, marriage pronouncement and kiss, closing remarks, and recessional. The proceedings can take anywhere from mere minutes to hours to days. But rest assured that if all you want to do is exchange the simplest of vows and get on with the rest of your life, that is certainly your prerogative.

The order in which the bridal party makes its way down the aisle—if there is an aisle—can also vary from wedding to wedding. But in almost all instances the

The daughter of the bride escorts her mother down the aisle (above left).
The path and sequence of the bridesmaids (above right) should be clarified well ahead of time. Quell children's jitters by reviewing instructions before the ceremony (opposite). The most important thing to tell them: Smile!

bride appears last. Traditionally, she is escorted by her father. Today, it is often both parents who have this honor. Sometimes it's a sibling or trusted friend; in the case of a second marriage, it may be an adult child of the bride.

What follows—the vows, readings, and musical interludes—is deeply personal and powerful, the means through which you can express your world view, how you see love, life, and marriage. Many couples write their own vows or amend traditional ones to reflect their expectations of the future and what they mean to each other. If yours is an interfaith marriage, decide which rituals from the two traditions you wish to incorporate. Take advantage of the months before the wedding to find passages and poems and listen to favorite songs that are emotionally true and important to you both.

Taking your vows may be serious business, but don't let anything keep you from enjoying the moment. Interact with the officiant in a comfortable, respectful manner. If you garble a vow or drop a ring, don't get flustered. Try laughing instead—this is *your* day.

And when the walk back down the aisle as husband and wife begins, let it be accompanied by the most uplifting, grand piece of music you can find.

A beautiful setting for the exchange of wedding vows (opposite). For a religious ceremony, an elaborate chuppah (below left) and ceremonial wine glass (below right) are prepared for the special day.

The Receiving Line

THE TRADITION OF THE RECEIVING LINE is a courtesy that guarantees each guest a few moments face-to-face with the bride and groom. It is an opportunity for them to meet the parents of the newlyweds, and gives the couple a chance to thank them for traveling from far and wide to share this day.

But for the happy new husband and wife, a receiving line with even just seventy-five guests can become a blur of air kisses and handshakes. For guests, it may just feel like . . . well, waiting in line. If you decide to have one, be sure that it's strategically placed and well organized. Start either at the end of the aisle at the exit of the ceremony space or at the entrance to the reception. If the ceremony and the reception are to be in the same place, locate the line far enough away so the caterers can set up for the reception.

Typically, the receiving line consists of the couple and their parents, although it can be whittled down to just the couple; speediness is a consideration, as this is a moment where many weddings lose momentum. Even with as few as thirty guests, each of whom spends three minutes with the couple and their parents, a receiving line can take way too long. Guests' energy levels (to say nothing of your own) might start to flag. Many couples find creative ways to move things along. One bride requested that a friend help by performing the introductions, thus politely limiting the amount of time each guest could spend with the wedding party. Another tempted people along by placing a waiter with a tray of Champagne and sparkling water at the end of the line but just far enough away so that guests wouldn't stop and talk there.

Some couples decide against having a receiving line altogether, instead hosting a light cocktail gathering after the service and before the reception. This allows guests a chance to start socializing with Champagne and petits fours while giving the bride and groom a more relaxed setting in which to welcome them.

For small weddings that are short on space, an informal personal greeting from the bride and groom is just as gracious as a receiving line.

The Celebration

FROM HERE ON, treat yourself as a guest. Let go of the planning details you've worked on so diligently for the last several months and allow the professionals and delegates to run the show. Remember: None of the guests know what plans you made, and all of them are there to have a good time; minor slip-ups or complications will go unnoticed. This is an intensely rich—and fleeting—moment in your lives. Don't waste it fretting.

The reception may be the first time extended family members are meeting one another. Make sure to facilitate introductions and nurture the development of these new relationships.

When guests arrive, they will pick up their seating assignments or place cards, drop off any gifts, and sign the wedding book if they didn't before the ceremony.

Find ways to spend quality time with guests during a cocktail hour before the reception (opposite). A dramatic dining tent set up with one long banquet table is the highlight of the evening (below).

By the time the receiving line is over, they're going to be hungry. It is crucial to serve them immediately upon their arrival at the reception. Hors d'oeuvres, punch, and Champagne should be passed right away; at the same time, guests should be directed to the bar and any standing food stations.

A relaxed cocktail hour before guests head to their tables should last an hour to an hour and a half. If you've hired a band or disc jockey, they might not be scheduled until the meal. Playing upbeat background music during this time will help people unwind. The main meal, whether a buffet or sit-down dinner, should be allotted at least an hour and a half. The bride and groom are usually served first to give them time to visit each table after they've finished dining.

Pacing, as always, is essential. Every reception has interruptions that guests look forward to and that move the party along, including toasts or announcements, the first dance, the cutting of the cake, the removal of the garter, and the bouquet toss. Your families' heritages and religious backgrounds may add their own traditions to the event.

The music should encourage guests to change dancing partners frequently (opposite). Guitarists add an element of fun and romance to any party (below left). Even the pool is decked out with wedding finery (below right).

Toasts and Good Wishes

TOASTS AND SPEECHES throughout a reception bestow blessings on the new husband and wife, give thanks, and mark the significance of their event. They can be poetic, funny, moving or didactic. Having friends perform these duties, rather than a bandleader or disc jockey, sounds a more personal note and is likely to better capture guests' attention.

 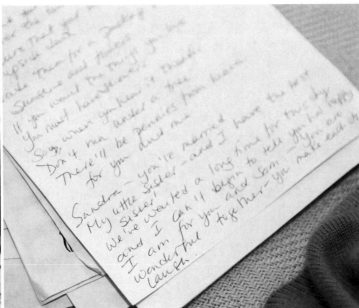 

The reception's first toast is usually given by the father of the bride after guests are seated and before the appetizer is served. (In the past, the groom was the first to speak, but this is less common today.) Speaking as the host of the event, he thanks his guests for coming and welcomes the groom's relatives into the bride's family. He might reminisce about his daughter as a little girl or talk about what makes the newlyweds' relationship unique and give his blessing for their future.

A round of other toasts is led by the best man, either before or after the meal. It is his role

Toasts and speeches allow friends and relatives to wax nostalgic and give blessings, thank you's, congratulations, and good wishes. The father of the bride raises a welcome toast to his guests (opposite).

to welcome guests, thank both sets of parents, and discuss his personal relationship with the bride and groom. Then he hands the floor over to the new couple, who thank families and friends for their support and for their presence at this event. If you aren't going to write your own vows, this time will give you an opportunity for more personal expression. Feel free to reminisce about the first time you met, to outline the history of your relationship (briefly and with discretion), and to reiterate the love you share. You might also read passages from the Bible, favorite books, poems, or songs.

After this, anyone is free to speak. Encourage variety—if you know a family member to be a terrific wit, don't be afraid to ask him to propose a toast. Encourage brevity, too: Too many toasts can destroy the forward motion of a party; it's not a bad idea to delegate an emcee if your guests are a voluble bunch. On the other hand, friends and members of the bridal party can be "planted" to keep toasts going in the event of a lull.

Everyone is welcome to take the floor. This is the couple's chance to acknowledge all those people who helped in the planning and preparations, and to thank those who played supportive roles in their lives.

The First Dance

FINALLY. THREE MINUTES ENTWINED in each other's arms. The first dance is a welcome time-out for the newlyweds, an extended embrace in the middle of a great deal of socializing. Soak it in.

The bride and groom traditionally share the first dance, alone on the dance floor, often to "their song." Learning how to dance for your wedding is a nice idea, but if all you know how to do is hug and sway to the music, by all means do just that without being self-conscious. Dance with confidence and concentrate on your new life partner, not on the fact that people are watching. If you see no need for a first dance, simply invite guests onto the dance floor when the music begins.

After the couple's first dance, the bride usually dances with her father and the groom with his mother. Other guests are welcome to cut in now or take the floor with each other.

Together at last! The first dance is not just representative of a couple's union, it's also a chance to hold each other in their arms, blow off steam, and show off nimble moves.

Cutting the Cake

A WEDDING CAKE ISN'T ONLY a gastronomic delight; it's part of a ritual that seals a marriage, and in some cultures is symbolic of fertility. The cutting of the cake by both the bride and groom occurs toward the end of the reception. It is important to keep this on schedule as this is also a signal to guests that the party will soon be ending. Some weddings include a groom's cake, which was traditionally included as a way to offer more than one kind of confection. But whether you have one cake or two, the ritual of cutting the bride's cake remains the same: The bride takes the knife (sometimes a family heirloom), the groom puts his hand over hers, and together they cut the first piece, which they then feed to one another. (Don't be tempted to smash a piece in your spouse's face—that's better left to television sitcoms!)

Wedding cakes can be complex concoctions as well as sweet confections. Rule of thumb for cutting one: Take a slice from the bottom tier. The bride holds the knife handle, the groom clasps her hand.

Happily Ever After

WHEN YOU LEAVE YOUR RECEPTION, you're stepping out into your future as husband and wife—and often away to a great honeymoon as well. This passage is frequently marked by a shower of confetti, birdseed, or flower petals (rice is not environmentally friendly and so should not be used). Close friends may have decorated your getaway car, so don't count on slipping away unnoticed. Traditionally, newlyweds make their exit before the party is over, in part as a cue to guests that the festivi-

ties are winding down, and making them feel comfortable about leaving as well.

Today, a lot of couples stay for the entire party instead of leaving early. This seems especially appropriate at a wedding at home, where it's often the parents of the bride or groom who are the hosts. And it's hard to leave a great party when your closest friends and family are still in a celebrating mood!

A departure might include a sea of bubbles, fancy transportation, flowers, and confetti. The bride's bouquet toss traditionally signals the beginning of the end of the party—though many brides choose to hold on to their flowers as a keepsake.

Real HOME WEDDINGS

❦ IN THE PROCESS OF interviewing so many helpful brides, grooms, and wedding professionals for this book, the editors came across countless real-life examples of truly perfect home weddings—perfect because they conveyed the individual taste of the couple and the joy of the occasion. In the following pages, we've highlighted eight real-life weddings that managed to gracefully reflect, through their choice of location, food, and decoration, the unique personal styles and spirituality, family histories, and regional identities of the newlyweds. ❦

ON THE *Beach*

LEE ELLEN BRETZ and W. Christopher Georgs were married on Torch Lake in Eastport, Michigan before two hundred guests. The land on which the wedding was held was settled by her great-grandfather.

- Timbers cut from behind the family house created a solid ceremonial focal point at the water's edge.

- The floral mix in baskets on top of the posts was composed of wildflowers, Queen Anne's lace, flox, and daisies picked on the property. An arch fashioned from grapevines, also found on their land, framed the ceremony.

- Elements from Christopher's family were incorporated into the celebration: his mother's pearl bracelet, worn by Lee; crystal flutes for toasts by the wedding party; and an image of a compass rose (signifying their love of sailing) appeared on invitations, centerpieces, and cufflinks given to the groomsmen.

- A silk satin runner in the same fabric as Lee's gown was used on a portable-floor aisle, which served as a stable walkway across the sand.

The day was a brilliant one for a ceremony under a wide blue sky. Instead of a formal receiving line, Lee and Christopher stood at the water's edge and greeted guests during an informal cocktail hour.

The bridal party posed in front of a barn built by Lee's great-grandfather (top left). Their navy blue attire— dark blue blazers with khaki trousers and deck shoes for the men, a choice of one of four designer dresses selected by the bride for the bridesmaids—was in keeping with the wedding's nautical theme. Following the ceremony, white wine was served on the beach (bottom left).

"I'd prepared myself for a monsoon. With a home wedding, you take a leap of faith."

LEE

Lee and Christopher hired a wedding coordinator for the day of the wedding to ensure that everything ran smoothly. Because of potentially high winds coming off the water, they opted for a frame tent with anchors and a plastic portable floor (right). The rental company added a special touch: They spray-painted the stakes and ropes crisp white the night before.

HEARTLAND
Vows

AFTER EXCHANGING VOWS in a small church in Wooster, Ohio, Amy Burger and Christopher Gamper celebrated their September nuptials with a sunset dinner for one hundred thirty-five in a barn on her parents' twenty-seven-acre farm.

At midnight the night before the wedding, a neighboring farmer and his wife arrived with a wagonload of pumpkins and gourds they had picked for the occasion. Amy, Christopher and their families joined them in decorating the barn and tent until two in the morning.

Though the reception was primarily outdoors, guests were welcome in the house as well. One room was outfitted with a baby bassinet for the youngest guests.

Hosting an elegant wedding in an unfinished barn meant starting from scratch. Electricity was installed and the space aired out for months in advance. Twinkle lights, luxe ribbons, dried hydrangea, and grapevines spruced up the wooden beams.

A small barn, dressed up with zinnias, apples, and corn cobs, served as the caterer's station (top left). The bridesmaids' bouquets (center left) were picked from a sea of miniature sunflowers on the farm, planted to reach full bloom the day of the nuptials (bottom left). Flowerpots planted with herbs were placed throughout the dinner site (opposite). Rosemary and ivy topiaries graced the tabletops, and "romance bulbs" of narcissus made the perfect party favors.

Top left: Because there wasn't enough room in the barn for the more than one hundred guests and a spacious dance floor, a tent served as an extension. Younger guests sat inside so they could enjoy the music, while those who preferred a more sedate setting sat outside.

"It was thrilling to be married in my hometown. Everyone knew about the wedding and chipped in or dropped by. That, besides my husband, was the best part." AMY

The newlyweds wowed friends with a skillful fox-trot for their first dance (bottom left), the result of months of "secret" dancing lessons. An eight-piece band playing swing tunes added dash to the bucolic setting (right).

FROM THE *Terrace*

GERI GREENLEE and Matthew Hooks wanted an intimate outdoor ceremony; the walled-in limestone terrace behind her mother's house in suburban Austin provided the perfect setting. An elegant sit-down dinner for fifty followed indoors.

The guest list was limited, partly so Geri could use the china her grandfather had bought for her expressly for her wedding.

Loose white flowers were scattered on the terrace and in its fountain and man-made stream.

After sunset, candles clustered in candelabra in the window nooks and on top of the walls provided much of the light.

Because they couldn't include all their friends in such a small party, Geri and Matthew threw a large, informal reception the following evening at a nearby wildflower center.

The outdoor wedding (top left) was a reflection of the couple's love of nature and of Matthew's proposal, an elegant sunrise Champagne toast atop a mountain. Geri's bouquet was a simple cluster of tuberoses, Matthew's favorite flower (bottom left). She wore her mother's diamond earrings and carried a scarf borrowed from Matthew's mother. A candelabra that belonged to her grandmother and namesake served as a backdrop to the ceremony (opposite).

The living room furniture was removed to make space for five rental tables and a dance floor (opposite). A white and gold color scheme prevailed. The table settings were a balance of high and low, with a short, lush arrangement of full-blown roses and tall, thin tapers. China, silver, and serving pieces belonged to the bride's family; glasses, napkins, and tablecloths were rented.

"Entertaining in the home is the most gracious and personal thing to do. Because of that, and the fact that we had this gorgeous setting in my mother's home, we never really considered other options."

GERI

Fresh flowers adorned the wedding cake, which was decorated by their florist and wedding designer (above right). Guests tossed rose petals at the couple as they stepped out into their new life together (below right).

GOTHAM
Romance

CONNIE CONNORS and Michael Fleisher invited one hundred twenty guests to their wedding. It was held on a late February afternoon in the living room of their still-unfurnished New York City loft—the quintessential urban party.

Bistro seating gave the living room a sophisticated air.

The couple borrowed the loft across the hall so they and the caterers would have a place in which to get ready. Couches moved into the hallway kept guests from feeling confined to one room.

The cast of the musical *Rent* accepted the bride's invitation to sing in place of the traditional recessional hymn.

Left, top to bottom: Handrolled honeycomb candles lined the windowsills. After some musical chairs, a sit-down dinner was served in the same room as the ceremony. The wedding cake was a replica of the couple's new home. A chuppah of sheer fabric edged with garlands of greenery for the Jewish-Catholic ceremony was hung from the ceiling over the mantel (opposite).

L. A. Love *Story*

Alanna Stang and András Szántó were married at Alanna's parents' home, some seven thousand miles from Budapest, where András grew up.

- Aisle chairs were adorned with bundles of lilies, and a garland of greenery suspended between two sycamore trees became a natural canopy for the ceremony.

- One hundred guests filed through the house for the receiving line, then out to the front lawn for cocktails.

- Meanwhile, the lawn was transformed into the reception area. Fully set tables were whisked from the back of the house, and ceremony chairs were repositioned.

- Candied violets embellished the wedding cake in remembrance of András's grandmother, an acclaimed baker who adorned her cakes with the same flowers.

Modern surroundings were softened by fanciful touches, such as votive candles on wrought-iron stakes staggered at various heights among the impatiens (above). Alanna's contemporary dress was offset by a blue enamel necklace that belonged to her mother and grandmother and a veil that was passed down through several family weddings (opposite).

Against the backdrop of a modern Los Angeles home in an unusually rustic setting, essential elements were carefully chosen and emphasized by the absence of extraneous decoration. Left, top to bottom: Alanna held a bouquet of white peonies. Both parents escorted her down the aisle. Candles in hurricane lamps were a spare, elegant touch that transformed the patio into a stage.

"With a garden wedding, we felt less pressure to conform to convention. Marrying at home allowed us a more personal experience than we would have had in a church or hotel."

ANDRÁS

Opposite: A judge officiated, and a friend of the couple's, a philosopher and art critic, spoke about the decision to marry at a time when couples are no longer compelled to do so for religious, financial, or social reasons. During the procession, a harpist played a selection of classical sonatas in lieu of the traditional wedding march.

Simple white table settings and minimalist centerpieces allowed the food to take center stage (opposite top). Tall vials of lilies embellished with a single gold bow made for elegant arrangements. The newlyweds enjoyed a private moment at the head table (opposite bottom left). Alanna removed her veil before dinner, but put it back on for one last photograph (opposite bottom right).

"The one thing I absolutely wanted for my guests was a great feast. I cared more about the food than the flowers." ALANNA

Right, top to bottom: Inside the garage, which was converted into a fully equipped kitchen, caterers prepared an elaborate meal that included lobster ravioli, Chilean sea bass, and berries brûlée in a sabayon-Champagne sauce. A lemon leaf and delicate ribbon graced each place setting. Tables were arranged in a horseshoe around the dance floor; heaters scattered throughout helped take the nip out of the May evening air. A Latin jazz band played till midnight.

ROSE GARDEN *Wedding*

CHARMAINE Curvan and Grant Lawes wanted to be married in a garden setting; they found the perfect one in her parents' backyard in suburban Toronto. The wedding took place on a late August afternoon; the guest list numbered one hundred thirty-five.

A rented trellis was placed on a green outdoor carpet, which was scattered with rose petals.

Because the tent was rented for the entire weekend, the bride's family also hosted a brunch the day after the wedding.

Charmaine and Grant used their own crystal glasses, which were decorated with a twist of ribbon for the party.

The bride's bouquet was composed mostly of white roses (above left), which echoed those grown in her father's garden. The bridesmaids' brilliant red dresses (above right) were chosen to match the vibrancy of the flowers in the backyard. The ceremony took place under perfect skies; a lacy wrought-iron trellis framed the wedding party and officiant (opposite).

"We arranged the chairs in
a horseshoe around us. It
was like we created a circle
of love for our service."

CHARMAINE

Charmaine, Grant, and the bridal party sat
at a banquet table festooned with tulle
and presided over by a rose wreath (above).
The evening's music was an eclectic mix,
with calypso reflecting the bride's
Trinidad and Tobago heritage (right), and
pop, reflecting the groom's British roots.

WESTERN *Classic*

BRANDY SIMMONS and William Archer, both native Texans, were married in May on her family's two thousand-acre ranch near Austin, where elk, guinea fowl, and peacock roam with horses bred for the rodeo. Four hundred guests attended.

❖ Six cowboys dressed in rodeo attire and on horseback greeted guests at the gates of the ranch and showed them to the parking area.

❖ Bridesmaids were brought to the ceremony tent in a flatbed borrowed from a wildflower center. The groom, ushers, and guests were ferried over in golf carts. Brandy and her father made the trip in a horse-drawn carriage.

❖ In keeping with the graceful, no-frills lay of the land, the couple had bundles of daisies placed throughout the wedding site, and chose simple white tulips for the bridal bouquet.

❖ Something old: Tucked into Brandy's garter belt was William's baby bonnet.

Daisies, symbolic of innocence and simplicity, were everywhere: marking the aisle and the ceremonial focal point (top left), embroidered on Brandy's gown and strewn across the carriage that transported her father and her to the ceremony (center left and opposite), even woven into the mane of the horse that pulled it. William's slick black cowboy hat was a gift from his future father-in-law (bottom left).

The bride wore traditional white, the groom wore classic "Texas tails": tuxedo jacket, black tie, jeans, and boots (opposite). The guests wore whatever they wished; no dress was specified on the invitations. The upbeat music of a mariachi band near the receiving line greeted guests on their way to the reception (top right).

"I'll never forget crossing that field in the carriage, people turning to watch us approach. My heart leapt in my chest. My father just kept squeezing my hand."

BRANDY

The barn turned out to be the perfect place for a wedding celebration (bottom right). The bleachers and stage were removed, and a platform and artificial turf were laid out. To create a warmer, dressier feel, soft white lights were draped over the dance floor. Guests kicked up their heels to country music, and the newly-weds showed off a nimble Texas two-step for their first dance.

SEASIDE
Nuptials

MIA SMEDEN AND BOB Matthews were married on a late October afternoon on Nantucket. After the church ceremony, the couple and their one hundred seventy-five guests enjoyed a two-tent reception.

A bagpiper led the guests from the church to Bob's home, where a martini bar was set up for a cocktail reception. The whole house was decorated in swags of chiffon.

A seafaring theme, inspired by a painting owned by the groom, was carried through both tents. The smaller, less formal tent was used for cocktails.

The formal dinner tent was covered in three thousand yards of tulle. Even the stairs leading to the tent were swagged and decked with the aisle markers from the ceremony.

The groom seemed totally at ease (top left). A horse-drawn carriage pulled the bride and her father through the cobblestone streets to the church (bottom left). Opposite, clockwise from left: Mia and her father posed for a photo before the ceremony while the flower girl and ring bearer set off on foot. The wedding's nautical theme was inspired by this Ralph Cahoun painting. The youngest member of the bridal party received congratulations for a job well done.

Loose floral arrangements, seashells, generous swags, and sheets of tulle lent a relaxed, natural feel to the formal dinner tent. Large bows marked the newlyweds' special dinner chairs (top left). Instead of bearing numbers, each table was named after a spot on the island, which was calligraphied on a seashell picture frame (bottom left).

"The little details made this wedding more memorable than the choice of chicken or beef. We placed touches of the sea and Nantucket in every corner. Even if only one person noticed, that's all that mattered."

MIA

Opposite: Tables were dressed with informal rose bouquets; tall tapers in shell-filled crystal candle holders distinguished the head table. Shimmery sheer organza squares were laid over the tablecloths; napkin holders were made of seashells and ribbon. All guests received miniature porcelain Nantucket baskets filled with chocolate shell candy.

At a decidedly fun-filled party, Bob and Mia flirted furiously with each other during the garter toss (opposite top). A remarkable sand castle wedding cake sent a message not to take things too seriously—even if you're wearing an antique tiara (opposite bottom left); a mermaid topper in the likeness of the couple sits on top (opposite bottom right).

"The overall effect was whimsical and elegant. You create the effect you want to by not worrying about how it's *supposed* to be done. You have to break the rules to make something memorable."

MIA

Mia's sister made a photo collage of the newlyweds (top right). After the ceremony, while guests enjoyed an informal reception at Bob's house, the couple took the horse-drawn carriage to the beach for photographs and a few quiet minutes before the party (bottom right).

Photo Credits

Photos are listed top to bottom, left to right, or clockwise from top left.

Front cover: Holger Thoss, Holger Thoss, Luciana Pampalone, William Stites

Back cover: Jim Bastardo

Jacket flap: Robert George, Luciana Pampalone, Joe Buissink

Case: Luciana Pampalone

Endpapers: front, Jason Walz; back, Holger Thoss

1 Luciana Pampalone

2 Joshua Ets-Hokin, Tanya Lawson, Tanya Lawson, Luciana Pampalone, Holger Thoss, Luciana Pampalone, Tanya Lawson, Joe Buissink, Joe Buissink

5 Holger Thoss

6 Holger Thoss, John Dolan, Holger Thoss

7 Holger Thoss, Holger Thoss, Cheryl Klauss

8 Holger Thoss

11 Tanya Lawson, Jeremy Saladyga–Gruber Photographers, Tanya Lawson, Holger Thoss, Tanya Lawson, Jason Walz, Holger Thoss, Tanya Lawson, Robert George

12 Julie Skarratt, Tanya Lawson, Jason Walz, Susan Bloch, Holger Thoss

15 Jason Walz, Valerie Shaff, Holger Thoss, Kaija Berzins Braus, Michelle Pattee

16 Stephane Colbert, Jeremy Saladyga–Gruber Photographers, Holger Thoss

17 (all) Jim Johnson

18 (all) Tanya Lawson

19 Tanya Lawson

20 Luciana Pampalone

21 (all) Tom Chute

23 (all) Marlene Wetherell

24 Terry deRoy Gruber–Gruber Photographers

25 Luciana Pampalone, Michelle Pattee

27 (all) Luciana Pampalone

28 Tanya Lawson, Phil Kramer

29 Julie Skarratt

31 Julie Skarratt, Frank Lopez, Terry deRoy Gruber–Gruber Photographers, Maria Fielding–Gruber Photographers, Joe Buissink, Stephane Colbert, Joe Buissink, Terry deRoy Gruber– Gruber Photographers, Holger Thoss

32 Valerie Shaff

33 Julie Skarratt

34 Kaija Berzins Braus

35 Jason Walz

36 John Dolan, Terry deRoy Gruber–Gruber Photographers

37 Tanya Lawson

39 Cary Hazlegrove

41 Robert George

42 Julie Skarratt, Stephane Colbert, Jason Walz

43 William Stites

44 Cary Hazlegrove

45 Phil Kramer, Tanya Lawson

47 Tanya Lawson, Frank Lopez, Holger Thoss, Luciana Pampalone

48 Terry deRoy Gruber–Gruber Photographers

49 Todd France–Gruber Photographers, Terry deRoy Gruber–Gruber Photographers

50 Kaija Berzins Braus, Terry deRoy Gruber–Gruber Photographers

51 Stephane Colbert

52 William Stites, Luciana Pampalone, William Stites

53 Tanya Lawson, William Stites

54 Marlene Wetherell, Susan Bloch

55 Kaija Berzins Braus, Joe Buissink, Joe Buissink, Jason Walz, Luciana Pampalone

57 William Stites, Jason Walz, Terry deRoy Gruber–Gruber

Photographers, Phil Kramer, Cary Hazlegrove, Joe Buissink

58 Luciana Pampalone

59 Luciana Pampalone, Keith Trumbo, Luciana Pampalone

60 (all) Jason Walz

61 Terry deRoy Gruber–Gruber Photographers

62 Jeremy Saladyga–Gruber Photographers, Maureen Edwards DeFries

63 Terry deRoy Gruber–Gruber Photographers

64 (all) Marlene Wetherell

65 Luciana Pampalone

66 Tanya Lawson, Jason Walz

67 Reportage, Inc.

68 Frank Lopez, Kaija Berzins Braus

70 Todd France–Gruber Photographers, Joe Buissink

71 Frank Lopez, Stephane Colbert, Tanya Lawson

72 William Stites

75 Maria Fielding–Gruber Photographers, Julie Skarratt, Luciana Pampalone, Joe Buissink, Diana Sanchez

76 Holger Thoss

77 Maria Fielding–Gruber Photographers, Luciana Pampalone

78 Holger Thoss, Joe Buissink

79 Kaija Berzins Braus

81 Cheryl Klauss, Valerie Shaff, John Maher–Gruber Photographers, Maria Fielding–Gruber Photographers, Jason Walz, Tanya Lawson, Holger Thoss, Holger Thoss, Luciana Pampalone

82 Holger Thoss, Joe Buissink, John Dolan, Jason Walz

85 Luciana Pampalone

86 Luciana Pampalone, Tanya Lawson

87 (all) Tanya Lawson

88 Luciana Pampalone,

Principal Photographers

Terry deRoy Gruber

Terry deRoy Gruber heads Gruber Photographers, Inc., a photography company representing Gruber and ten other photographers of weddings and special events. His work has appeared in *Vogue*, *Vanity Fair*, *Martha Stewart Living*, *People*, and *Bride's*.

Luciana Pampalone

Luciana Pampalone has been a freelance photographer for over ten years. Her work has appeared in *Victoria*, *Country Living*, and several books. She lives in New York City with her husband.

Holger Thoss

New York–based Holger Thoss approaches wedding photography with the same sensibility and personal vision that influence his other commercial and personal projects. He is very happily married.

Tanya Malott Lawson

Wedding and fashion photographer Tanya Lawson travels worldwide for great celebrations. Since 1991, she has been photographing clients in the arts, society, and business. Her work has been published in *Town & Country*, *Martha Stewart Living*, *Bride's*, and *The New York Times*.

Stylist

Marlene Wetherell

Marlene Wetherell has worked as a fashion, still-life, and interiors stylist for the past twelve years. Her work has appeared in various publications. Recently, she has turned her styling talents towards photography. Her photographic work has appeared in *Victoria*, *Architectural Digest*, and *Southern Accents*.

Credits

Resources

Beauty

Kimara Ahnert
1113 Madison Ave.
New York, NY 10028
212.452.4252
makeup

Peter Anthony Studio
Park City, UT
801.649.9595
full-service salon

C.O. Bigelow Chemists
414 Avenue of the Americas
New York, NY 10011
212.473.7324
www.bigelowchemists@msn.com
skin-care products

Bliss Spa
568 Broadway
New York, NY 10012
212.219.8970
www.blissworld.com
full-service salon; mail order

Body Serene Day Spa
4007 Skippack Pike
Skippack, PA 19474
610.584.7284
www.thebodyserene.com

Boyd's
655 Madison Ave.
New York, NY 10021
212.838.6558
www.boydsnyc.com
cosmetics, makeup artists

**Brownes & Company
Apothecary**
841 Lincoln Rd.
Miami Beach, FL 33139
305.532.8784
plant-based skin-care supplies, cosmetics, makeup applications; mail order

Michael Christopher Salon
5441 Mayfield Rd.
Lyndhurst, OH 44124
440.449.0999

Susan Ciminelli Day Spa
754 West 58th St.
New York, NY 10019
212.872.2650
www.susan-ciminelli.com
full-service spa; skin-care, massage

City Salon
118 Newbury St.
Boston, MA 02116
617.236.4990

Jacques Dessange
45 E. Oak St.
Chicago, IL 60611
800.9.SALONS 312.951.6270
773.395.8578
hair

Nelson D' Leon Designs
50 West 34th St.
New York, NY 10001
212.563.9879
bridal hair, makeup; by appointment

Garren at Henri Bendel
712 Fifth Ave.
New York, NY 10019
212.841.9400
full-service hair salon

Laura Geller Makeup Studio
1044 Lexington Ave.
New York, NY 10021
212.570.5477
www.laurageller.com
hair and makeup

Jolie the Day Spa
3619 Piedmont Rd.
Atlanta, GA 30305
404.266.0060
full-service spa, aromatherapy, massage

Kiehl's Pharmacy
109 Third Ave.
New York, NY 10003
800.KIELS1
212.475.3698
hair and skin-care products, cosmetics; call for local availability

Ronni Kolotkin
New York, NY
212.366.6663
electrolysis; by appointment

Lachapelle Representation Ltd.
420 East 54th St.
New York, NY 10022
212.838.3170
hair and makeup artists' representatives

La Dolce Vita Spa and Salon
927 E. Broadway
Long Beach, CA 90802
562.432.3760
www.ladolcevitaspa.com

Mariana's Skin Care
498 Elliot St.
Beverly, MA 01915
978.922.0707
www.marianaskincare.com
makeup, facials, body treatments

Minardi Salon
29 East 61st St., 5th Floor
New York, NY 10021
212.308.1711
full-service hair and beauty salon specializing in hair color

**Natural Retreat Salon
& Day Spa**
8730 Taub Rd.
Houston, TX 77064
281.970.1100

Pavlova Day Spa
114 S. Union St.
Traverse City, MI 49684
616.941.5707
hair, nails

Phoenix, The
5600 W. Lovers Lane, Suite 100
Dallas, TX 75209
214.352.8411
hair styling and cosmetics

Kathy Pomerantz
New York, NY
212.772.3865
makeup; by appointment

Salon Cristophe
1125 West 18th St.
Washington, DC
202.785.2222
hair salon, makeup artists

Salon Levante
Nikki Knutson
3040 Hennepin
Minneapolis, MN 55403
612.827.3699
hair, makeup

Salon on Sutter
560 Sutter St., Suite 200
San Francisco, CA 94102
415.986.8266

Scentiments & Essentials at Fred Segal
500 Broadway
Santa Monica, CA 90401
310.394.8509
beauty products, fragrances, cosmetics

Sephora
555 Broadway
New York, NY 10012
212.625.1309
www.sephora.com
makeup

Stan Milton Salon
721 Miami Circle, Suite 102
Atlanta, GA 30024
404.233.6242

Strawberry Jam
44C S. Main St.
New Hope, PA 18938
215.862.9251
fragrances, cosmetics

Studio Benjamin Robin
4930 Sherbrook St. West
Westmount, Quebec H3Z 1H3
514.485.9672

30 Newbury Day Spa
30 Newbury St., 4th Floor
Boston, MA 02116
617.437.7775

Valerie Beverly Hills
460 N. Cannon Dr.
Beverly Hills, CA 90210
800.282.5374
makeup; by appointment

Yosh for Hair
Gina Khan
173 Maiden Lane
San Francisco, CA 94108
415.989.7704

Zano Salon and Spa
1767 W. Ogden Ave.
Naperville, IL 60540
630.778.8999

Cakes

Ann Amernick
2516 University Blvd. West
Wheaton, MD 20902
301.718.0434
301.933.1517

Ashley Bakery
Charleston, SC
843.763.4125

August Thomsen Corporation
Glen Cove, NY
800.645.7170
cake-making supplies; catalog

Ayoma Cake Masterpieces
Toronto, ON
416.225.9442
www.weddinguide.com/pages/ayoma

Ron Ben-Israel Cakes
42 Greene St.
New York, NY 10013
212.625.3369
www.weddingcakes.com
by appointment

Bijoux Doux Specialty Cakes & Pastries
304 Mulberry St.
New York, NY 10012
212.226.0948

Margaret Braun
New York, NY
212.929.1582
sugar objects, trompe l'oeil jeweling
a specialty; by appointment

Broadway Panhandler
477 Broome St.
New York, NY 10013
212.966.3434
French bakeware, cake pans,
decorations

Cake Art Supplies
1512 Fifth Ave.
San Rafael, CA 94901
415.456.7773

Cake Decorating by Toba
New York, NY
212.234.3635

Cake Gallery
1508 Roswell
Marietta, GA 30062
770.578.0339

Cakery
5151 S. Federal Blvd.
Littleton, CO 80203
303.797.7418
fondant a specialty

Cakes and Cookies by Maria
240 Willow Rd., RR1
Walnutport, PA 18080
610.767.7109
custom cakes

Cake Shoppe
832 Sheppard Ave. West
Downsview, ON M3H 2T1
416.638.2253

Cakes to Remember
248 Cypress St.
Brookline, MA 02445
617.738.8508
www.townandcountry.com
by appointment

Cakeworks
Los Angeles, CA
213.934.6515
tromp l'oeil portraits; by appointment

Susan Kennedy Chopson
644 Delaware Ave.
Madison, TN 37115
615.865.2437
by appointment

Classic Cakes
Indianapolis, IN
317.844.6901

CMW Enterprises
Christine Hasler
Ontario
905.823.1560

Colette's Cakes
681 Washington St.
New York, NY 10014
212.366.6530
sugar work, sculptural creations; by
appointment

Columbus Bakery
959 First Ave.
New York, NY 10022
212.421.0334

Cravings
8149 Big Bend Blvd.
Welster Groves, MO 63119
314.961.3534
buttercream a specialty

Cupcake Cafe
522 Ninth Ave.
New York, NY 10018
212.465.1530

Diane's Bakery
23 Bryant Ave.
Roslyn, NY 11576
516.621.2522

Les Friandises
972 Lexington Ave.
New York, NY 10021
212.988.1616
patisserie, custom cakes

Frosted Art by Arturo Diaz
1546 Edison St.
Dallas, TX 75207
214.760.8707
pastillage flowers, groom's cakes

Le Gateau Cakery
3128 Harvard Ave.
Dallas, TX 75205
214.528.6102

Hansen Cake
1072 S. Fairfax Ave.
Los Angeles, CA 90019
323.936.4332

Beth Hirsch Baking Company
3 York St.
New York, NY 10013
212.941.8085
miniature cakes

Fran Jacobs Pastry
40 Avenue B
New York, NY 10016
212.614.9054
fondants, petits fours

**Paul Jerabek Special Affairs
Catering**
5010 Elsby Ave.
Dallas, TX 75209
214.351.3607
custom cakes, buttercream

**Jessica's Cakes for Weddings &
Other Celebrations**
Eden Prarie, MN
612.829.0673

John and Mike's Amazing Cakes
14934 NE 31st Circle
Redmond, WA 98052
425.869.2992
architectural and theme cakes

John Paul's Creative Cakes
1255 Belvedere Dr.
North Charleston, SC 29406
843.744.6791
by appointment

Cheryl Kleinman Cakes
448 Atlantic Ave.
Brooklyn, NY 11215
718.237.2271
Wedgwood cakes; by appointment

Tin Larsson
Sag Harbor, NY
516.725.2318
private chef; custom cakes

New French Bakery
122 N. Fourth St.
Minneapolis, MN 55401
612.341.9083
also tortes

**New York Cake & Baking
Distributors**
56 West 22nd St.
New York, NY 10011
212.675.2253
www.nycake.com

Nutcracker Sweet Shop
508 Kerrwood Rd.
Pittsburgh, PA 15215
412.963.7951

**Parrish's Cake Decorating
Supplies**
Gardena, CA
310.324.CAKE

Patisserie Lanciani
414 West 14th St.
New York, NY 10014
212.989.1213

Patticakes Dessert Company
1900 N. Allen Ave.
Altadena, CA 91001
626.794.1128
by appointment

Ana Paz Cakes
1460 NW 107th Ave., Unit D
Miami, FL 33172
305.471.5850
custom designer

La Petite Fleur
Jan Kish
633 Oxford St.
Worthington, OH 43085
614.848.5855
cakes, marzipan fruits, favors,
brochures; by appointment

Piece of Cake
1035 Johnnie Dodds Blvd., Suite B9
Mt. Pleasant, SC 29464
843.881.2034

Pink Rose Pastry Shop
630 S. Fourth St.
Philadelphia, PA 19147
215.592.0565

Polly's Cakes
Portland, OR
503.230.1986
www.pollyscakes.com
custom cakes; by appointment

Queen of Hearts
Terry Karpen
69 Dayton Rd.
Redding, CT 06896
203.938.3578

Michel Richard
310 S. Robertson Blvd.
Los Angeles, CA 90048
310.275.5707

Rosemary's Cakes
Rosemary Littman
240 Rutland Ave.
Teaneck, NJ 07666
201.833.2417

Le Royale Icing by Margaret Lastick
35 Chicago Ave.
Oak Park, IL 60302
708.386.4175
custom cakes

Katrina Rozelle Pastries and Desserts
5931 College Ave.
Oakland, CA 94618
510.655.3209
fondant a specialty; by appointment

Sima's
817 North 68th St.
Milwaukee, WI 53213
414.257.0998

Smith's One of a Kind Edible Art
12823 S. Regal St.
Traverse City, MI 49684
616.922.2336

SUD Fine Pastry
801 E. Passyunk Ave.
Philadelphia, PA 19147
215.592.0499

Sugar Bouquet by Rosemary Watson
23 N. Star Dr.
Morristown, NJ 07960
800.203.0629
973.538.3542

Sweet Lady Jane
8360 Melrose Ave.
Los Angeles, CA 90069
323.653.7145

Sweet Sisters
157 Fifth St.
Clifton, NJ 07011
973.478.2650
www.angelfire.com/nj/sweetsisters
by appointment

Taste of Europe by Gisela
4817 Brentwood Stair
Fort Worth, TX 76103
817.654.9494
www.atasteofeurope.com

Thomas Wedding Cakes
27811 Five Mile Rd.
Livonia, MI 48154
734.427.9050

Thomas Wedding Cakes
27811 Five Mile Rd.
Livonia, MI 48154
734.427.9050

Three Tarts
301 S. Happ Rd.
Northfield, IL 60093
847.446.5444

Betty van Norstrand
6 Leonard Rd.
Poughkeepsie, NY 12601
914.471.3386
hand-painted miniature sugar
work a specialty

Victoria's Fancy Wedding Cakes
Minneapolis, MN
612.853.0011

Gail Watson Custom Cakes
335 West 38th St.
New York, NY 10018
212.967.9167
pastillage, buttercream; by appointment

Wedding Cakes by Meribeth
Raleigh, NC
919.846.5454

Sylvia Weinstock Cakes
273 Church St.
New York, NY 10013
212.925.6698
by appointment

Debra Yates
5418 NW Venetian Dr.
Kansas City, MO 64151
816.587.1095
marzipan a specialty

Caterers

All in Good Taste
1520 Monteray St.
Pittsburgh, PA 15212
412.321.5516

Avant Grill Catering Company
4636 South 36th St.
Phoenix, AZ 85040
602.243.7100
www.theavantgrill.com

Christine Bib Catering
Toronto, ON
416.533.6832

Black Tie Events
Phoenix, AZ
602.249.7999

Bonbonerie
2030 Madison Rd.
Cincinatti, OH 45208
513.321.3399

Bonne Bouche Catering
Capitola, CA
831.479.9637

Margo Bouanchaud, Inc.
5744 Capitol Hieghts Ave.
Baton Rouge, LA 70806
225.952.9010

Walter Burke Catering
Santa Fe, NM
505.473.9600

Cabbages & Kings Catering
Westport, CT
203.226.0531
catering & event planning

Cake & Company
San Francisco, CA
415.346.0989
by appointment

Calla Lily
92 Kirkland St.
Cambridge, MA 02138
617.492.2545

Capers Catering
Arlington, MA
781. 648.0900
800.465.6509
www.caperscatering.com

Catered Affair
Hingham, MA
781.982.9333
www.thecateredaffair.com

Catering Company
Kansas City, MO
816.444.8372

City Farm
5 Kendall St.
Brookline, MA 02445
617.566.6683

Coup de Gras Catering
2923 N. Milwaukee Ave.
Chicago, IL 60618
800.683.6446
www.coupdegras.com

Laurence Craig Distinctive Catering & Event Management
1799 Springfield Ave.
Maplewood, NJ 07040
973.761.0190

Creative Edge Parties
Carla Ruben
110 Barrow St.
New York, NY 10014
212.741.3000
www.creativeedgeparties.com

Culinary Arts
6100 4th Ave. South
Seattle, WA 98108
206.768.0677

Custom Catering by Larry
2800 Olive
St. Louis, MO 63103
314.531.4111

East Meets West Catering
560 Harrison Ave., Suite 107
Boston, MA 02118
617.426.3344

Eat Smart Cafe Catering
Boston, MA
978.658.7790
healthful catering

Elegant Catering
14424 North 32nd St.
Phoenix, AZ 85032
602.482.3334

Epicurean Catering
6022 S. Holly St.
Greenwood Village, CO 80111
303.770.0877

Farrelli's Catering
14848 N. Cave Creek Rd., Suite 18
Phoenix, AZ 85032
602.905.7200

Food for All Seasons
124 W. Summit
Ann Arbor, MI 48103
734.747.9099
www.foodforallseasons.com

Susan Gage Caterer
7411 Livingston Rd.
Oxon Hill, MD 20745
301.839.6900

Glorious Food
Sean Driscoll
504 East 74th St.
New York, NY 10021
212.628.2320

Good Gracious!
Pauline Perry
5714 W. Pico
Los Angeles, CA 90019
323.954.2277

Great Performances
287 Spring St.
New York, NY 10012
212.727.2424
www.greatperformances.com
on-site caterers at Wave Hill

Heck's
4555 Renaissance Parkway, Suite 103
Warrensville, OH 44128
216.464.8020

Susan Holland Company
142 Fifth Ave., 4th Floor
New York, NY 10011
212.807.8892
www.susanholland.com

Joel's Grand Cuisine
3930 Euphrosine St.
New Orleans, LA 70125
800.335.8994
www.joels.com

Katherine's Catering
359 Metty Dr., Suite 4
Ann Arbor, MI 48103
734.930.4270
www.katherines.com

Wendy Krispin Caterer
1025 N. Stemmans, Suite 600
Dallas, TX 75207
214.748.5559

Juli Lieberman Fine Catering
2008 S. Lincoln St.
Arlington, VA 22204
703.892.3770
www.finecatering.com

Manhattan Caterers
7960 Winston St.
Burnaby, BC V5A 2H5
604.421.2711

Susan Mason, Inc.
206 W. Gaston St.
Savannah, GA 31401
912.233.9737

Ruth Meric Catering
3030 Audley
Houston, TX 77098
713.522.1448

Occasions by Kimberly
2128 Losantiville Rd.
Cincinatti, OH 45237
513.351.9009

Patricia's Weddings & Custom Cakes Unlimited
1009 Jefferson Ave.
Reading, OH 45215
513.733.3100
serving Ohio, Indiana, and Kentucky

Proof of the Pudding
2033 Monroe Dr.
Atlanta, GA 30324
404.892.2359
www.proofatlanta.com

Ritz Charles
12156 N. Meridian
Carmel, IN 46032
317.846.9158

Robbins Wolfe Eventeurs
Christopher Robbins
521 West St.
New York, NY 10014
212.924.6500
516.671.2127
www.robbinswolfe.com

Ruins, The
570 Roy St.
Seattle, WA 98109
206.285.7846

Sammy's
1400 West 10th St.
Cleveland, OH 44113
216.523.5899
www.partyperfect.net

Sargeant's
6317 Murry Lane
Brentwood, TN 31027
615.373.9331

Sensational Host
3030 Route 73 North
Maple Shade, NJ 08052
609.667.5005

**Sharon's Custom
Designed Cakes**
1334 Benton St.
Crete, IL 60417
708.672.6722
www.sharonscakes.com

Special Occasions Catering
5341 25th Ave. NE
Seattle, WA 98105
206.527.1253
www.nwwedding.com

**Lewis Steven's Distinctive
Catering**
811 W. Deer Valley Rd.
Phoenix, AZ 85027
623.580.8111
www.lewisstevens.com

Sweet Surrender
3522 12th St. NE
Washington, DC 20017
202.529.6331

Taste of Excellence
7830 Freeway Circle
Middleburg Heights, OH 44130
440.891.5968

Tiffaney's Catering Ltd.
13020 Delf Place
Richmond, BC V6V 2A2
604.207.1221
www.tiffaneys.com

Upper Crust
4401 Kiln Court
Louisville, KY 10218
502.456.4144

Windows Restaurant
Phil Murray
7677 W. Bayshore Dr.
Traverse City, MI 49684
616.941.0100

Word of Mouth
919 West 12th St.
Austin, TX 78703
512.472.9500
888.474.9673
call for consultation

Wuollet Bakery
3608 West 50th St.
Minneapolis, MN 55405
612.546.7007

David Ziff Cooking
New York, NY
212.289.6199

Consultants and Event Designers

All About Weddings
Newman, GA
770.463.9990

Elizabeth K. Allen, Inc.
New York, NY
212.289.4931

Along Came Mary
Los Angeles, CA
323.931.9082
www.alongcamemary.com

Avatar Event Planning
Rodney Gray
New York, NY
212.686.8381

Preston Bailey
New York, NY
212.691.6777

Beautiful Memory
Boulder, CO
303.499.0959
www.geocities.com/paris/lights/2058

Marcy Blum Associates
New York, NY
212.688.3057

Gary Bravard Event Design
Indianapolis, IN
317.687.1920
www.garyevents@aol.com

Celebrations
Memphis, TN
901.525.5223

Collections
Indianapolis, IN
317.283.5251

Creative Parties
Bethesda, MD
301.654.9292

Event Design with Panache
Duluth, GA
770.476.7129

Event of the Year
New York, NY
212.807.0907
location service

Fabulous Weddings
New York, New Jersey &
Connecticut
877.508.1772
www.fabulousweddings.com

Marsha Heckman
Mill Valley, CA
415.388.2295
wedding consultation and
floral design

Peter Helburn
Just Ask Peter
Aspen, CO
970.925.3351

Hopple Popple
Linda Matzkin
Newton, MA
617.964.6550

Connie Keyrns, Bridal Network
California
510.339.3370

Michelle Lally
Pittsburgh, PA
412.731.2028

Neal A. Matticks
New York, NY
212.874.8930
event planner and floral designer

PAM Associates
Patricia Martel
Northern Michigan
231.599.2911

Rafanelli Events
Boston, MA
617.357.1818

Lynne Schlereth
18 South Terrace
Short Hills, NJ 07078
973.379.5627

Gale Sliger Productions
Dallas, TX
214.637.5566

Takashimaya New York
New York, NY
212.350.0100
www.takashimaya.com

Tansey Design Associates
Bill Tansey
232 West 30th St.
New York, NY 10001
212.594.2287
by appointment

Anthony Todd
New York, NY
212.367.7363

Wedding Library
Vancouver, BC
604.683.1670

Weddings by Jordan
Atlanta, GA
770.962.5190

Mindy Weiss
Beverly Hills, CA
310.205.6000

Winslow Associates
Greenwich, CT
203.869.6612
specializing in home weddings

Fashion

Alençon
318 Miller Ave.
Mill Valley, CA 94941
415.389.9408
custom gowns

Altobello Fine Jewelers
361 Town Square
Wheaton, IL 60187
630.871.9000

Amsale
625 Madison Ave.
New York, NY 10022
800.765.0170
212.971.0170
www.amsale.com
gowns; call for local availability

Anakha
New York, NY
212.367.8051
gowns; by appointment only

Angel Threads
Brooklyn, NY
718.246.0551
www.angelthreadsnyc.com
accessories, linens; catalog

John Anthony Salon
153 East 61st St.
New York, NY 10021
212.888.4070
gowns, shawls

Aricie Lingerie de Marque
50 Post St.
San Francisco, CA 94104
415.989.0261

Chris Arlotta Enterprises
183 Madison Ave.
New York, NY 10016
212.779.0711
foundations, corsetry; call for local availability

Helene Arpels
470 Park Ave.
New York, NY 10021
212.755.1623
shoes, evening slippers, accessories

Auer's
210 Saint Paul St.
Denver, CO 80206
303.321.0404
gowns

B&J Fabrics
263 West 40th St.
New York, NY
212.354.8150
chantilly lace, silk specialties

Barney's New York
9570 Wilshire Blvd.
Beverly Hills, CA 90212
310.276.4400
Vera Wang collection, accessories

Bearlace Cottage
412 Marsac
Park City, UT 84060
435.649.8804
heirloom lace and antique gowns

Bebe Elegante
3338 N. Ashland Ave.
Chicago, IL 60657
773.477.2323
flower girl dresses, boys' tuxedos

Bella Donna
539 Hayes St.
San Francisco, CA 94102
415.861.7182
custom gowns, veils, shoes

Bell'occhio
8 Brady St.
San Francisco, CA 94103
415.864.4048
vintage ribbon, silk flowers

Henri Bendel
712 Fifth Ave.
New York, NY 10019
212.247.1100

Bergdorf Goodman
754 Fifth Ave.
New York, NY 10019
212.753.7300
full-service salon

Camilla Dietz Bergeron, Ltd.
818 Madison Ave.
New York, NY 10021
212.794.9100
antique and estate jewelry

Christian Bernard
201.330.1007
jewelry; 20 locations

Gina Bianco
New York, NY
212.924.1685
textile and gown conservation and restoration, custom headpieces

Biltmore Estate's Gatehouse Gift Shop
Biltmore Estate
Asheville, NC
800.968.0358
828.274.6220
accessories; catalog

Birnbaum & Bullock
New York, NY
212.242.2914
custom gowns; by appointment

Manolo Blahnik
31 West 54th St.
New York, NY 10019
212.582.3007
shoes; call for local availability

La Boutique des Brides
888 Brannan St., #1195
San Francisco, CA 94103
415.431.3400

Boutique Nuptiale
6534 Saint Hubert St.
Montreal, Quebec H25 2M3
514.277.4296

Bowdon Designer Fashions
250 Healdsburg Ave.
Santa Rosa, CA 95448
707.433.9405
gowns

Bridal & Formal
300 W. Benson St.
Cincinatti, OH 45215
513.821.6622
gowns

Bridal Basics
1475 Buford Dr., Suite 403-108
Lawrenceville, GA 30043
770.237.0545
gowns

Bridal Couture and Evening Wear
8220 N. Hayden, Suite C-108
Scottsdale, AZ 85258
602.991.3207
www.bridalcouture.com
gowns

Bridal Salon at Stanley Korshak
500 Crescent Court, Suite 142
Dallas, TX 75201
214.871.3611
full service salon; wedding consultant

Bridals by Franca
11725 North 19th Ave.
Phoenix, AZ 85029
602.943.7973
gowns; by appointment

Bride, The
230 Newport Center Dr.
Newport Beach, CA 92660
949.760.1800

BRIDES by Peggy Barnes
2031 Post Oak Blvd.
Houston, TX 77056
713.622.2298
www.cyberbride.com
gowns

Bride's Collection
Nancy Issler
Princeton, NJ
732.438.0099
gowns

Bride's House
1010 Locust St.
St. Louis, MO 63101
314.621.1833

Brides to Be
Tempe, AZ
480.831.6017
gowns

Brimar, Inc.
Northbrook, IL
708.272.9585
metallic cording, tassels; call for local availability

Britex Fabrics
146 Geary St.
San Francisco, CA 94108
415.392.2910
www.britexfabrics.com
vintage buttons

Sydney Bush
New York, NY
212.563.8023
traditional bridal lingerie; call for local availability

Joan Calabrese
4930 Westchester Pike
Edgemont, PA 19028
212.967.4767
flower girl dresses; call for local availability

Capezio Dance Theatre Shop
1650 Broadway
New York, NY 10019
212.245.2130
ballet slippers; catalog

Châlloner, NYC
399 W. Broadway
New York, NY 10012
212.274.1437
headpieces, gloves, handbags; call for local availability; by appointment

Chanel
15 East 57th St.
New York, NY 10022
212.688.5055
couture

Alan Cherry Bridal
55 Avenue Rd.
Toronto, ON M5R 3L2
416.922.7433
gowns

Joy Cherry Bridal
3323 Yonge St.
Toronto, ON M4N 2L9
416.489.8809
gowns

Christina's Bridal
5200 S. Archer
Chicago, IL 60632
773.581.8200
dresses, shoes, invitations

Cinderella
60 West 38th St.
New York, NY 10018
212.840.0644
ribbons, trimmings, silk flowers; catalog

Clay Pot
162 Seventh Ave.
Brooklyn, NY 11215
800.989.3579
718.989.3579
www.clay-pot.com
wedding bands, jewelry; catalog

Clea Colet
960 Madison Ave.
New York, NY 10021
212.396.4608
gowns; by appointment; call for local availability

Cobblestone Rose
101 S. Ann Arbor Rd., Suite 1
Saline, MI 48176
734.944.6202
veils, headpieces

Kenneth Cole
95 Fifth Ave.
New York, NY 10003
800.KEN.COLE
212.675.2550
shoes; catalog available

Collection on Park Avenue
501 Park Ave. South
Winter Park, FL 32789
407.740.6003
gowns

Coup de Chapeaux
1821 Stiener St.
San Francisco, CA 94115
415.931.7793
www.coupdechapeaux.com
custom design and vintage hats,
millinery restoration

La Crasia
304 Fifth Ave.
New York, NY 10001
212.594.2223
www.wegloveyou.com
custom gloves

Kathleen Crowley
San Fransisco, CA
415.864.5616
gowns

**Angela Cummings Boutique
at Bergdorf Goodman**
754 Fifth Ave.
New York, NY 10019
212.872.8874
wedding bands, jewelry

Cupid's Garden
185 N. Robertson Blvd.
Beverly Hills, CA 90211
310.360.0256
www.cupidsgarden.com
gowns

Donald Deal
202 West 40th St., 12th Floor
New York, NY 10018
212.398.5007
www.donalddeal.com
gowns; available at Saks Fifth Avenue,
Nieman Marcus, Bergdorf Goodman;
by appointment in showroom

Leslie DeFranesco
Brooklyn, NY
718.965.1085
flat ribbonwork creations; by
appointment

Designs on You
545 Sutter St., Suite 304
San Francisco, CA 94102
415.956.0130

Dessy Creations
1345 Broadway
New York, NY 11018
800.337.7911
informal gowns; call for local
availability

Olga D'Gallegos, Inc.
52 Seventh Ave., Penthouse
New York, NY 10018
212.921.0049
gowns; showroom; call for local
availability

Christian Dior
800.807.7701
414.328.3211
call for local availability

Dolce & Gabbana
660 Madison Ave., 10th Floor
New York, NY 10021
212.966.2868
contemporary gowns; call for local
availability

Lily Dong Couture Bridal
Cupertino, CA
408.255.8850
www.lilydongcouture.com

Amy Downs
New York, NY
212.598.4189
custom hats

Dream Veils and Accessories
676 N. Deerborne
Chicago, IL 60610
312.943.9554

Linda Dresner
484 Park Ave.
New York, NY 10022
212.308.3177
299 W. Maple Rd.
Birmingham, MI 48009
248.642.4999
custom gowns

Elements Jill Schwartz Ltd.
343 Main St.
Great Barrington, MA 01230
413.644.9994
www.elementsjillschwartz.com
custom jewelry; call for local
availability

Endrius
New York, NY
212.838.5880
custom couture gowns;
by appointment

Escada USA
Hasbrouck Heights, NJ
800.869.8424
call for local availability

Bob Evans
10 East 38th St., 3rd Floor
New York, NY 10016
212.889.1999
custom gowns; call for local availability

Exclusives for the Bride
311 W. Superior, Suite 216
Chicago, IL 60610
312.664.8870
gowns; by appointment

Hang Fen
333 West 39th St., 12th Floor
New York, NY 10018
212.695.9509
gowns, shawls, handbags

Fenorali for Regalia
28 Summer St., 4th Floor
Boston, MA 02210
617.723.3682
www.regaliaveils.com
veils, shoes, other accessories

Alberta Ferretti
New York, NY
212.460.5500
Available at Saks Fifth Avenue,
Barney's, Bloomingdale's, Dillard's,
Nordstrom

Fino Fino
Allied Arts Guild
75 Arbor Rd.
Menlo Park, CA 94025
650.321.8720
www.finofino.com
custom veils

Florals to Formals
3135 Fernbrook Lane North
North Plymouth, MN 55447
612.473.5608
gowns

Shawn Ray Fons
498 Seventh Ave., 24th Floor
New York, NY 10018
212.967.7979
custom bridal; by appointment

Carrie Forbes
Los Angeles, CA
602.367.9236
crocheted evening bags

Forget Me Knots
1738 Union St.
San Francisco, CA 94123
415.921.0838
bridesmaid dresses, bridal accessories,
wedding favors

Formal Affair
1441 Arapahoe Ave.
Boulder, CO 80302
303.444.8294

Formally Yours Bridal Boutique
11550 Gravois Rd.
St. Louis, MO 63126
314.849.1144
gowns

Forsyth Enterprises Ltd.
Delray Beach, FL
561.266.0400
www.evahforsyth.com
gowns; designer, manufacturer

Peter Fox Shoes
105 Thompson St.
New York, NY 10011
212.431.7426
catalog

Framm Ltd.
2667 Main St.
Santa Monica, CA 90405
310.392.3911
vintage and custom gowns

Gardener's Ribbons & Lace
2235 E. Division
Arlington, TX 76011
817.640.1436
vintage and one-of-a-kind ribbons

Gentle Arts
4500 Dryads St., Suite B
New Orleans, LA 70115
504.895.5628
textile restoration, specializing in lace

Giordano's
1150 Second Ave.
New York, NY 10021
212.688.7195
shoes, sizes 4–6 only

Givenchy Bridal
212.223.4646
call for local availability

Amy Jo Gladstone
Long Island City, NY
718.706.0300
custom boudoir slippers, silk creations

Richard Glasgow
New York, NY
212.683.1379
couture gowns; call for local availability

Les Habitudes
101 N. Robertson Blvd.
Los Angeles, CA 90036
310.273.2883
contemporary romantic fashions

Handmade Veil
8900 Blossom Dr.
Cincinatti, OH 45236
513.793.7701

Hannelore's Bridal Boutique
423 King St.
Alexandria, VA 22314
703.549.0387
www.hannelores.com

Marlene Harris Collection
238½ Freeport Rd.
Pittsburgh, PA 15238
412.828.1245
www.marleneharriscol.com
antique jewelry

Hat Shop
120 Thompson St.
New York, NY 10012
212.219.1445

Carolina Herrera
501 Seventh Ave.
New York, NY 10018
212.944.5757
custom gowns; call for local availability

Herschelle Couturier
101 Jessie St.
San Francisco, CA 94105
415.982.0112
custom evening wear and gowns

Homa Bridal
Millburn-Short Hills, NJ
973.655.1239
veils, headpieces, other accessories

B. Hughes Bridal and Formal
4231 Harding Rd.
Nashville, TN 37205
615.292.9409
gowns

Christopher Hunt Designs
224 West 35th St., Suite 1310
New York, NY 10001
212.244.0420
custom gowns, formal attire for men;
by appointment

Shanneen Huxham at Metropolitan Design Group
80 West 40th St.
New York, NY 10018
212.944.6110
handmade gloves & bags; call for
availability

Jeanne's Fantasia
611 Millwood Blvd.
Nashville, TN 37205
615.352.1726
traditional and contemporary gowns,
headpieces

Sandra Johnson Couture
138 S. Robertson Blvd.
Los Angeles, CA 90048
310.247.8206
couture

Maria Jung Couturier
370 Miracle Mile
Coral Gables, FL 33134
305.461.2090
custom gowns; by appointment

Kalima
135 West 12th St.
New York, NY 10012
212.691.9520
gowns; by appointment

Yumi Katsura Bridal House
907 Madison Ave.
New York, NY 10021
212.772.3760
www.yumikatsura.com
gowns; by appointment

Hamilton Kennedy at Takashimaya
693 Fifth Ave.
New York, NY 10022
212.350.0100
lingerie

Pat Kerr
200 Wagner Place
Memphis, TN 38103
901.525.5223
heirloom lace bridal gowns; by
appointment; call for local availability

Marina Killery Couture Hats
New York, NY
212.639.9277
custom straw hats; by appointment

Jenny Kim Couture
5200 W. Loop South, #300
Houston, TX 77401
713.592.0373
call for appointment

Kleinfeld
8282 Fifth Ave.
Brooklyn, NY 11209
888.838.2777
718.833.1100
gowns

Ann Lawrence Antiques
801 Early St.
Santa Fe, NM 87501
505.982.1755
antique gowns

Legacy
109 Thompson St.
New York, NY 10012
212.966.4827
gowns

Stéphanie Lesaint Haute Couture
150 Newark St.
Hoboken, NJ 07030
201.792.0208
couture and custom gowns; by appointment

Kenneth Lily
16301 Raymer St.
Van Nuys, CA 91406
818.785.5626G
gowns and accessories

Lola Millinery
New York, NY
212.219.1445
hats; call for availability

Lord West
5707 31st Ave.
Woodside, NY 11377
800.275.9684
tuxedos for women; call for availability

Rene Mancini
212 West 35th St.
New York, NY, 10001
212.761.0121

M&J Trimming
1008 Sixth Ave.
New York, NY 10008
212.391.9072
http://mjtrim.com
notions, custom millinery

Manny's Millinery Supply
26 West 38th St.
New York, NY 10018
212.840.2235
hat boxes, petticoats, notions, veiling; sewing; catalog

Mary Ann Maxwell for the Bride
5906 Rose St. at Westcott
Houston, TX 77007
713.802.1100
bridesmaid dresses; event planning

May Arts
1154 E. Putnam Ave.
Riverside, CT 06878
203.637.8366

Tia Mazza
New York, NY
212.989.4349
handmade crowns, veils; call for local availability

Belle Meline
New York, NY
516.473.1039
veils

Midori Ribbon
3524 W. Government Way
Seattle, WA 98199
206.282.3595
organza, silk ribbons; call for local availability

Mika Inatome
11 Worth St., Suite 4B
New York, NY 10013
800.22.INATO
www.inatome.com
gowns; call for local availability

Mikimoto
730 Fifth Ave.
New York, NY 10020
212.586.7153
pearls, jewelry

Badgley Mischka
525 Seventh Ave., 14th Floor
New York, NY 10018
212.921.1585
gowns; call for local availability

Mona's Bridal Boutique
1110 N. Hacienda Blvd.
La Puente, CA 91744
626.917.9775

Mon Atelier
119 N. La Brea Ave.
Los Angeles, CA 90036
323.937.1189
custom gowns, tuxedos

Debra Morefield
466 Broome St.
New York, NY 10012
212.226.2647
ready-to-wear and custom alternative fashion

Patience Morgan Jewelry
Stony Point, NY
914.942.1894

Morgane le Fay
746 Madison Ave.
New York, NY 10021
212.879.9700
151 Spring St.
New York, NY 10013
212.925.0144
67 Wooster St.
New York, NY 10013
212.219.7672
1528 Montana Ave.
Santa Monica, CA 90403
310.393.4447
contemporary collection

Helen Morley Designs Ltd.
New York, NY
212.594.6404
www.helenmorley.com
gowns; call for local availability

Marina Morrison Ltd.
30 Maiden Lane
San Francisco, CA 94108
415.984.9360
www.marinamorrison.citysearch.com
gowns

Laura Morton Design
Los Angeles, CA
310.289.1166
bridal collection, wedding sets

Anthony Muto
200 West 20th St., Suite 808
New York, NY 10011
212.691.5598
custom bridal designs and consultation

Neiman Marcus
9700 Wilshire Blvd.
Beverly Hills, CA 90212
310.550.5900
gowns

Kathryn Nixon
New York, NY
212.979.8699
custom dressmaker

Vanessa Noel
12 West 57th St., Suite 901
New York, NY 10019
212.333.7882
www.vanessanoel.com
shoes; call for local availability

Obiko
794 Sutter St.
San Francisco, CA 94109
415.775.2882
gowns

One-of-a-Kind Bride
89 Fifth Ave., Room 902
New York, NY 10003
212.645.7123
gowns; by appointment

Out of the Past
9012 Third Ave.
Brooklyn, NY 11209
718.748.1490
antique fashions and accessories

Anita Pagliaro Ltd.
414 W. Broadway
New York, NY 10012
212.966.2200
gowns

Paris Hats & Veils
305 W. Benson St.
Cincinatti, OH 45215
513.948.8888
custom crowns, veils, tiaras;
catalog

Paris 1900
2703 Main St.
Santa Monica, CA 90405
310.396.0405
antique and restored gowns

La Perla
777 Madison Ave.
New York, NY 10011
212.570.0050
www.laperla.com
silk foundations; call for local
availability

**Prince and Princess
Children's Boutique**
33 East 68th St.
New York, NY 10021
212.879.8989

Po Couture
552 Seventh Ave., Penthouse
New York, NY 10018
212.921.0049
gowns and veils

Point Pavilion
620 Scott St.
Covington, KY 41011
606.491.9191
lingerie

Priscilla of Boston
137 Newbury St.
Boston, MA 02116
617.267.9070
www.priscillaofboston.com
gowns, headpieces, shoes; call for
local availability

Promenade Fabrics
1520 Saint Charles St.
New Orleans, LA 70130
504.522.1488
ribbons, fabrics

Rafael Jewelers
1200 Fourth St.
San Rafael, CA 94901
415.567.1925

Reinstein Ross
122 Prince St.
New York, NY 10012
212.226.4513
www.nytoday.com/reinsteinross
custom-designed jewelry, reproduction of ancient designs; call for local
availability

Reisinger Jewelers
36 E. Fourth St., Bartlett Building
Cincinatti, OH 45202
513.381.2002

Ribbonerie
191 Potrero Ave.
San Francisco, CA 94103
415.626.6184
wired, silk ribbons; call for local
availability

Ribbonry
119 Louisiana Ave.
Perrysburg, OH 43551
419.872.0073
www.ribbonry.com
ribbons, kits, book, accessories

**Ken Riney Antiques &
Estate Jewelry**
500 Crescent Court, Suite 154
Dallas, TX 75201
214.871.3640

Ristarose
1422 Grant Ave.
San Francisco, CA 94133
415.781.8559
gowns

Renee Romano
676 N. Deerborne
Chicago, IL 60610
312.943.0912
wedding veils and tiaras

Michelle Roth & Co.
24 West 57th St., Suite 203
New York, NY 10019
212.245.3390
www.michelleroth.com
exclusive European and American
gowns

Cynthia Rowley
112 Wooster St.
New York, NY 10011
212.334.1144
808 West Armitage Ave.
Chicago, IL 60614
773.528.6160
gowns

Brenda Schoenfeld
8319 Preston Center Plaza
Dallas, TX 75225
214.368.4007
custom wedding bands

Holly Sharp
3636 Pacific Coast Highway East
Corona del Mar, CA 92625
949.673.9466
gowns

Sigerson Morrison
242 Mott St.
New York, NY 10012
212.219.3893
shoes

Kevin Simon Clothing
1358 Abbot Kinney Blvd.
Venice, CA 90291
310.392.4630
custom gowns; by appointment

Tamara Smith Designs
Saratoga, CA
408.867.0598
jewelry

S.O.L.E.
Soledad Twombley
611 Broadway
New York, NY 10012
212.477.2005
gowns

**Something Old,
Something New**
1064 River Rd.
Edgewater, NJ 07020
800.RINGS.44
201.224.9224
wedding bands

Sopp
800.233.2697
hair ribbons; call for local availability

**Southern Heirlooms by
Edie Jordan**
305 N. Natchez St., Suite G
Kosciusko, MS 39090
601.289.5638
veils

Sposabella Lace
252 West 40th St.
New York, NY 10018
212.354.4729
fabrics, custom millinery, dressmaking

Walter Steiger
739 Madison Ave.
New York, NY 10021
212.570.1212
www.waltersteiger.com
shoes; call for local availability

Stubbs & Wooten
22 East 72nd St.
New York, NY 10021
212.249.5200
custom bridal for men and women;
boudoir slippers

Swarovski
New York, NY
800.289.4900
212.213.9001
fine Austrian crystal, handbags, jewelry;
call for local availability

Sweet Peas
8416 Third Ave.
Brooklyn, NY 11209
718.680.5766
flower girl dresses

Tatters
36 Broadway
Newport, RI 02840
401.841.0886
gowns, dresses; special order

Tender Buttons
143 East 62nd St.
New York, NY
212.758.7004
vintage buttons

Bêbê Thompson
1261 Lexington Ave.
New York, NY 10028
212.249.4740
flower girl fashions

Time After Time
8311½ W. Third St.
Los Angeles, CA 90046
323.653.8463
vintage bridal fashions

Tomasina
615 Washington Rd.
Mt. Lebanon, PA 15228
412.563.7788
www.tomasinabridal.com
custom gowns

Touch of Ivy
51 Everett Dr., Suite A50
Princeton Junction, NJ 08550
609.252.1191
cotton ribbon, gifts; call for local
availability

Toujours
2484 Sacramento St.
San Francisco, CA 94115
415.346.3988
www.toujourslingerie.com
bridal lingerie, hosiery, accessories

Trouvaille Française
New York, NY
212.737.6015
Victorian fashions, petticoats, linens,
laces; by appointment

Ulla-Maija
24 West 40th St.
New York, NY 10018
212.768.0707
couture gowns; call for local availability

Patricia Underwood
New York, NY
212.268.3774
hats; call for local availability

Vaban Gille
800.448.9988
imported silk, wired ribbons; call for
local availability

Alvina Valenta
Babylon, NY
516.661.0492
gowns; call for local availability

Viewpoint Showroom
John Hardy
14 East 38th St.
New York, NY 10016
800.254.2739
212.696.1881
www.viewpointshowroom.com
jewelry

Meryl Waitz
New York, NY
212.675.7224
www.merylwaitz.com
jewelry; call for local availability

Vera Wang Bridal House
991 Madison Ave.
New York, NY 10023
212.628.3400
212.575.6400
contemporary gowns, custom
couture; by appointment

Wearkstatt
33 Greene St.
New York, NY 10013
212.334.9494
contemporary and custom; by
appointment; call for local availability

Stuart Weitzman
New York, NY
212.582.9500
www.stuartweitzman.com
shoes; call for local availability

**Wedding Dress at
Saks Fifth Avenue**
611 Fifth Ave.
New York, NY 10021
212.940.2269
3440 Peachtree Rd.
Atlanta, GA 30326
404.261.7234
gowns; full-service salons

Wells-Ware
New York, NY
888.90.WELLS
212.222.9177
custom jewelry; wedding mementos

Jane Wilson-Marquis
155 Prince St.
New York, NY 10012;
212.477.4408
130 East 82nd St.
New York, NY 10028
212.452.5335
www.bridalgowns.com
couture bridal and evening wear

Margaret Wolfe
Los Angeles, CA
310.322.1397
hand-dyed ribbons, Victorian
ribbonwork

Zazu & Violets
1790 Shattuck Ave.
Berkeley, CA 94709
510.845.1409
made-to-measure straw hats

Zita's Bridal Design
1122 N. Aster
Milwaukee, WI 53202
414.276.6827

Floral and Garden Designers and Supplies

All Seasons Flowers
1399A Third Ave.
New York, NY 10021
800.435.0822
212.628.1280

Anthony Garden Boutique Ltd.
134 East 70th St.
New York, NY 10021
212.737.3303
by appointment

Arrangement
3841 NE Second Ave.
Miami, FL 33137
305.576.9922
by appointment

Atelier, a Workshop
3419 Milton Ave.
Dallas, TX 75205
214.750.7622
custom designs

Atlanta Flower Market
427 Roswell Rd.
Atlanta, GA 30328
770.396.3301

Avant-Gardens
9280 SW 40th St.
Miami, FL 33165
800.771.7150
305.554.4300

Baldwin Park Florist
14607 Ramona Blvd.
Baldwin, CA 91706
888.22.ROSES
626.337.7106

Philip Baloun Designs
340 West 55th St.
New York, NY 10019
212.307.1675

Baumgarten Krueger
225 E. Wisconsin Ave.
Milwaukee, WI 53202
414.276.2382
www.bkflorist.com

Beautiful Flowers
15 West 26th St., 6th floor
New York, NY 10010
212.686.5569
by appointment

L. Becker Flowers
217 East 83rd St.
New York, NY 10028
212.439.6001

Bloom
16 West 21st St.
New York, NY 10010
212.620.5666
www.bloomflowers.com

Bloomers
2975 Washington St.
San Francisco, CA 94115
415.563.3266

Blossoms
33866 Woodward Ave.
Birmingham, MI 48009
248.644.4411

Blue Meadow Flowers
336 East 13th St.
New York, NY 10003
212.979.8618
hand-wired bouquets; by appointment

Boston Blossoms
468 Commonwealth Ave.
Boston, MA 02215
888.417.7673
617.536.8600

Botanica
227 West 28th St.
New York, NY 10001
212.563.9013

Botanica
937 S. Cooper St.
Memphis, TN 38104
901.274.5767
architectural and naturalistic
garden styles

Botanicals on the Park
3014 S. Grand
St. Louis, MO 63118
800.848.7674
314.772.7674
www.botp.com

Bouquet Florists
5242 Port Royal Rd.
Springfield, VA 22151
703.321.8484

Bouquets
1525 15th St.
Denver, CO 80202
303.333.5500

Robert Bozzini
San Francisco, CA
415.351.2823

Brady's Floral Design
7625 E. Redfield Rd.
Scottsdale, AZ 85260
800.782.6508

Judith Brandley, Florist of Sierra Madre
Sierra Madre, CA
626.355.6972

David Brown Flowers
4622 Center
Houston, TX 77007
713.861.4048

Buckhead Florist
3333 Peachtree Rd. NE, Suite 100
Atlanta, GA 30326
800.665.9939
404.266.7426
www.buckheadflorist.com
call for consultation

Cactus Flower Florists
Phoenix, AZ
602.483.9200
800.924.2887
www.cactusflower.com

Calabria
New York, NY
212.675.2688

Carole Beautiful Flowers
717 Elm St.
Winnetka, IL 60093
847.446.7700

Carving Ice Productions
970 S. Orangethorpe, Suite C
Anaheim, CA 92801
714.871.7999

Castle & Pierpont
401 East 76th St.
New York, NY 10021
212.570.1284

C.C. Flowers
2 N. Central, Suite 150
Phoenix, AZ 85004
602.263.7671

Central Floral
40 West 28th St.
New York, NY 10001
212.686.7952
tools, supplies

Charleston Florist
184 King St.
Charleston, SC 29401
843.577.5691

Peter A. Chopin Florist
3138 Magazine St.
New Orleans, LA 70115
504.891.4455

Columbine Custom Flower Design
80 K St.
South Boston, MA 02127
617.269.6555

Lois Cremmins, Flowers
North Salem, NY
914.669.8272

Crest of Fine Flowers
417 Fourth St.
Wilmette, IL 60091
847.256.3900
by appointment

Stacey Daniels Flowers
42 Ganung Dr.
Ossining, NY 10562
800.463.7632
English garden style; by appointment

David Brothers Design
Dallas, TX
214.443.9935
by appointment

Devonshire
340 Fourth Ave.
Palm Beach, FL 33480
561.833.0796

Earth Blooms
2101 Abrams Rd.
Dallas, TX 75214
214.823.6222

Emilia's Floral
702 East & 123rd St. South
Draper, UT 84020
801.943.7301

English Garden
Nashville, TN
615.269.0197
by appointment

Susan Eshelman and Pei-Hsin Gedalesia
826 Country Club Dr.
Wooster, OH 44691
330.264.7981

Esprit de Fleur
Seattle, WA
206.533.9277
by appointment

Everyday Gardener
2945 Old Canton Rd.
Jackson, MS 39216
601.981.0273
garden accessories

Fiori
17 NE Fifth St.
Minneapolis, MN 55413
612.623.1153

Fleurish Flower Design
Lizzie Nylund
Cambridge, MA 02141
617.491.8376

Floral Décor by Ken & Lisa Gibbons
250 First St.
Jersey City, NJ 07301
201.217.0924
212.502.3485
dried flowers, topiaries

Florals of Waterford
74 E. Allendale Rd.
Saddle River, NJ 07458
201.327.0337
unusual combinations

Floral Trunk
4770 Banning Ave.
White Bear Lake, MN 55110
651.426.8989

Flora Nova
1302 NW Hoyt
Portland, OR 97209
503.228.1134

Floridella
1920 Polk St.
San Francisco, CA 94109
415.775.4065

Florist Grand
705 S. King St., Suite 100
Honolulu, HI 96813
808.599.4132

Florist on the Green
Allen N. Hermansson
2 West St.
Newtown, CT 06470
800.334.7673
203.426.6788

Flowers by Leah
Sunland, CA
818.353.0730

Flowers by Marcelle
2814 W. Bell Rd., Suite 1420
Phoenix, AZ 85053
800.221.6705
602.942.2892

Flowers on Chestnut
1 Chestnut St.
Nantucket, MA 02554
508.228.6007

Flowers on the Park
56 E. Sixth St.
St. Paul, MN 55101
651.227.2896

Flowersticks
47 N. Main St.
Falmouth, MA 02540
508.548.9776

Flowers Unlimited
1230 Eglinton Ave. West
Mississauga, ON L5V 1N3
800.787.7749
905.542.1500
www.flowersunltd.com

Foliage Garden
120 West 28th St.
New York, NY 10001
212.989.3089
www.foliagegarden.com
flowering plants, trees; for purchase
or rental

Ford's Flower & Nursery
4445 W. Tenth Ave.
Vancouver BC V6R 2H8
604.224.1341

Nancy Frank Flowers
377 Havana Ave.
Long Beach, CA 90814
562.498.6147
by appointment

Fresh Oregon Holly
St. Helens, OR
800.821.0172
fresh-cut holly; mail order

Friendly Floral Gallery
2208 Halloway St.
Durham, NC 27703
919.596.8747
www.friendlyfloralgallery.com

Ryan Gainey & Company
Atlanta, GA
404.233.2050

Gardener's Eden
San Francisco, CA
800.822.9600
garden supplies, containers, greenery;
catalog

Garden Gate Creative Design
2811 Routh St.
Dallas, TX 75201
800.646.5840
214.220.1272
hand-painted aisle runners

Garden Shop
246 Bellevue Ave.
Upper Montclair, NJ 07043
973.743.9736

Garden Store
678 South 700 East
Salt Lake City, UT 84102
801.595.6622

Glorimundi
307 Seventh Ave.
New York, NY 10001
212.727.7090
floral, event designer; by appointment

Curtis M. Godwin
New York, NY
212.645.2639

Grasmere
40 Maple Ave.
Barrington, RI 02806
401.247.2789

Grassroots Garden
131 Spring St.
New York, NY 10012
212.226.2662
plants, trees, supplies

Valorie Hart Designs
Sunnyvale, CA
408.720.9506
full-service planning, sculptural
designs

Hastings & Hastings
27 Miller Ave.
Mill Valley, CA 94941
415.381.1272

Hibiscus
10010 N. Executive Hills Blvd.
Kansas City, MO 64153
816.891.0808

Horticulture Design
David Madison
211 West 28th St., 3rd Floor
New York, NY 10001
212.629.7330

Elizabeth House
1431 South Blvd.
Charlotte, NC 28203
704.342.3919

Jennifer Houser
New York, NY
212.532.8676
Bridgehampton, NY
516.537.5532
by appointment

Indigo V.
1352 Castro St.
San Francisco, CA 94114
415.647.2116
by appointment

Robert Isabell, Inc.
410 West 13th St.
New York, NY 10014
800.617.7767
212.645.7767

Jacques Designs
269 S. Beverly Dr., Suite 366
Beverly Hills, CA 90212
310.859.6424

J.P. Floral Design
949 Wakefield Dr.
Houston, TX 77018
713.524.8311
www.jpfloral.com

Kinsman Company
Point Pleasant, PA
800.733.4146
www.kinsmangarden.com
complete line of garden accessories;
catalog

Kiybele Creations
41 Windmill Rd.
Armonk, NY 10504
914.273.6659
garden accessories; call for local
availability

Kristine Fleurs
Kristine Ellis
New York, NY
212.598.4130

David Kurio Floral Design
4302 Airport Blvd.
Austin, TX 78722
512.467.9947

Flowers by Frank Laning
400 King St.
Chapaqua, NY 10514
800.238.5258
914.238.5100

Larkspur
514 N. Third St.
Minneapolis, MN 55401
612.332.2140

Laurels Custom Florist
7964 Melrose Ave.
Los Angeles, CA 90046
323.655.3466

J. Levine Books & Judaica
New York, NY
800.553.9474
212.695.6888
www.levine-judaica.com
chuppahs; catalog

Flowers Tommy Luke
1701 SW Jefferson St.
Portland, OR 97201
503.228.3131

Joseph Maake Flowers & Decorative Accessories
Oyster Bay, NY
516.921.3076
fresh and dried flowers

Main Street Floragardens
San Anselmo, CA
415.485.2996
by appointment

Marsh Meadows Design
13214 Whitebluff Rd.
Savannah, GA 31419
912.925.9849

Meadowsent Florist
Gardner Gables
Rte. 4455
Gardner, NY 12525
914.255.3866

Mei Mei
New York, NY
212.631.3516
by appointment

A. Midori Floral Studio
2559 N. Scottsdale Rd.
Scottsdale, AZ 85257
602.413.0789

Miss Roger's Flower Shop
150 Route 6A
Orleans, MA 02653
508.255.0884
serving Cape Cod

Mitch's Flowers
4843 Magazine St.
New Orleans, LA 70115
504.899.4843

Munder-Skiles
799 Madison Ave., 3rd Floor
New York, NY 10021
212.717.0150
reproduction garden ornaments,
furniture; custom work

Nanz & Kraft Florist
141 Breckinridge Lane
Louisville, KY 40207
502.897.6551
www.nanzkraft.com

Nature's Daughter
Basking Ridge, NJ
908.221.0258
also event planning; by appointment

New England Garden Ornaments
38 E. Brookfield Rd.
North Brookfield, MA 01535
508.867.4474
www.negardenornaments.com
garden structure; catalog

Fred Palmer Flowers
2214 W. Alameda
Santa Fe, NM 87501
505.820.0044

Palmer-Kelly Floral Designs
5168 N. College Ave.
Indianapolis, IN 46205
317.923.9903

Andrew Pascoe Flowers
47 W. Main St.
Oyster Bay, NY
516.922.9561
by appointment; will travel

Paxton Gate
1204 Stevenson St.
San Francisco, CA 94103
415.255.5955
garden supplies, landscaping services

Perfect Petal
3615 West 32nd Ave.
Denver, CO 80211
303.480.0966

Portafiore
119 West 23rd St., Suite 405
New York, NY 10011
212.620.4038
by appointment

Potted Gardens
41 King St.
New York, NY 10014
212.255.4797
unusual containers

Prudence Designs
235 West 18th St.
New York, NY 10011
212.691.1356

Purple Iris Florist
7739 Northcross Dr.; Suite Q
Austin, TX 78757
800.333.9759
512.458.4747

Quailcrest Farm
2810 Armstrong Rd.
Wooster, OH 44691
330.345.6722

Charles Radcliff, the Florist
1759 Richmond Ave.
Houston, TX 77098
713.522.9100

Alexandra Randall Flowers
St. James, NY
516.862.9291

Rayon Vert Extraordinary Flowers
3187 16th St.
San Fransico, CA 94103
415.861.3516
floral design & decorative accessories

Regalo Flowers
151 Washington Ave.
Santa Fe, NM 87501
505.983.4900

Renae's Flowers & Gifts
1924 Martin Luther King Ave. SE
Washington, DC 20020
202.678.1785

Renny Design for Entertaining
505 Park Ave.
New York, NY 10022
800.RENNY10
212.288.7000

Rieko M.
619 S. Washington
Royal Oak, MI 48067
810.543.5433

Rosedale Nursery
51 Saw Mill Pkwy.
Hawthorne, NY 10532
914.769.1300
garden supplies, landscaping services

Rossi & Rovetti
365 W. Portal Ave.
San Fransisco, CA 94127
415.566.2260

Seasons: A Floral Design Studio
Gerald Palumbo
888 Eighth Ave.
New York, NY 10019
212.586.2257

**Silver Birches Custom
Design Floristry**
477 S. Raymond Ave.
Pasedena, CA 91105
626.796.1431

Smith & Hawken
394 W. Broadway
New York, NY 10012
800.776.3336
garden supplies; catalog, call for local
availability

Some Enchanted Evening
Phoenix, AZ
480.785.9668

Spring Street Garden
186½ Spring St.
New York, NY 10012
212.966.2015
by appointment

Spruce
75 Greenwich Ave.
New York, NY 10014
212.414.0588

Laurie Stern Floral Art
727 Sea View Dr.
El Cerrito, CA 94530
510.528.8040
Victorian and English country style;
by appointment

StoneKelly
328 Columbus Ave.
New York, NY 10023
212.875.0500

Ten Pennies Florist
1921 S. Broad St.
Philadelphia, PA 19148
215.336.3557

TFS
616 N. Almont
Los Angeles, CA 90069
310.274.8491
floral studio; vintage collectibles

Tommy Thompson
504 S. Main St.
Ann Arbor, MI 48103
734.665.4222

**Thru the Grapevine–
Elk Rapids**
10437 S. Bay Shore Dr.
Elk Rapids, MI 49629
800.864.7273

Thru the Grapevine–Petoskey
4237 Main St.
Bay Harbor, MI 49770
231.489.2796

**Christian Tortu at
Takashimaya**
693 Fifth Ave.
New York, NY 10022
212.350.0100
unusual combinations, containers

**Trochta's Flowers and
Greenhouses**
6700 N. Broadway
Oklahoma City, OK 73116
800.232.7307
405.848.3338

Mary Tuttle's Floral and Gifts
191 Lamp and Lantern Village
Town & Country, MO 63017
800.366.0480
314.394.0480

Van Bassen Flowers
2901 Bayview Ave.
Toronto, ON M2K 1E6
800.551.9810
416.222.6751

Vanderbuilt & Company
1429 Main St.
St. Helena, CA 94574
707.963.1010
baskets for indoors and out

Very Special Flowers
204 W. Tenth St.
New York, NY 10014
212.206.7236
full-service planning, sculptural
designs

Vine Floral
310 Vine St.
St. Catharines, ON L2M 4T3
800.710.9054
905.934.7134
www.ftd.com.vine

Waterford Gardens
Saddle River, NJ
201.327.0337
water lilies; water garden supplies

Ron Wendt Design
245 West 29th St., 5th Floor
New York, NY 10001
212.290.2428
garden style; by appointment

White House Nursery
52 Springfield Ave.
Berkeley Heights, NJ 07980
908.665.0775

Wild Child
333 Main St.
Wakefield, RI 02879
401.782.8944
www.sprig.net

Wildflowers of Louisville
500 S. Fourth Ave.
Louisville, KY 40202
502.584.3412

Wild Things
400 Maple Ave.
Oradell, NJ 07649
201.262.7701

Winston Flowers
Boston, Chestnut Hill, and
Wellsley, MA
800.457.4901
617.541.1101

Wisteria Design Studio Ltd.
275 Market St., Suite 50
Minneapolis, MN 55405
612.332.0633
www.wedstreet.com

Woods Exquisite Flowers
11711 Gorham Ave.
Los Angeles, CA 90049
310.826.0711

Yours Creatively
535 Wilson Heights Blvd.
North York, ON M3H 2V7
416.636.3341

Zezé Flowers
New York, NY
212.753.7767

Home Fashions

ABC Carpet & Home
888 Broadway
New York, NY 10003
212.473.3000
www.abchome.com
slipcovers, tableclothes, decorative
accessories, gifts, flowers

Alphapuck Designs
New York, NY
212.267.2561
slipcovers, tablecloths; custom work

Anichini
Turnbridge, VT
802.889.9430
www.anichini.com
fine linens; call for local availability

Annie Glass
109 Coopers St.
Santa Cruz, CA 95060
831.427.4260
gifts, glassware; bridal registry

Baccarat
800.363.4700
crystals and gifts; call for local
availability

Banana Republic
888.BRSTYLE

Meg Cohen Design
New York, NY
212.473.4002
silk and wool table scarves, silk
pillows; call for local availability

**Country Originals & The
Design Collection**
3844 N. Northside Dr.
Jackson, MS 39209
800.249.4229
601.366.4229
home accessories, gifts; catalog

Elizabeth Street Gallery
1176 Second Ave.
New York, NY 10021
212.644.6969
www.dir-dd.com/elizabeth-street.html
architectural remnants, garden
fixtures, sculpture

Françoise Nunnalle
New York, NY
212.246.4281
antique linens; by appointment

Garden Antiquary
724 Fifth Ave., 3rd Floor
New York, NY 10019
914.737.6054
iron, stone sculptures, antique
ornaments, fixtures, furnishings;
by appointment

Gardener, The
1836 Fourth St.
Berkeley, CA 94710
510.548.4545
unusual containers, handmade paper,
ceramics

Gargoyles
512 S. Third St.
Philadelphia, PA 19147
215.629.1700
www.gargoylesltd.com
collectibles and accessories to rent
and purchase

Paula Gins Antique Linens
7233 S. Sundown Circle
Denver, CO 80120
303.734.9095

Ann Gish, Inc.
California
805.498.4447
linens

Handcraft of South Texas
Pharr, TX
800.443.1688
wire containers; custom designs
available

Sue Fisher King
3067 Sacramento St.
San Francisco, CA 94115
415.922.7276
www.dellajarres.com
ceramics, linens, toiletries, gifts;
on-line gift registry

Leron Linens
750 Madison Ave.
New York, NY 10021
212.753.6700

Linen Gallery
7001 Preston Rd.
Dallas, TX 75205
214.522.6700

David Luke & Associate
773 14th St.
San Francisco, CA 94114
415.255.8999
antiques

Mackenzie-Childs Ltd.
824 Madison Ave.
New York, NY 10021
212.570.6050
linens

La Maison Moderne
144 West 19th St.
New York, NY 10011
212.748.9070
www.lamaisonmoderne.com
decorative objects; registry

Monticello Studio
1800 N. Rockwell Ave.
Chicago, IL 60647
773.227.4540
reproduction architectural objects,
columns, sconces, boxes; catalog

Nay Et Al By Nay
8844 W. Olympic Blvd., Suite B
Beverly Hills, CA 90211
301.273.5140
www.nayetaldesignsbynay.com
table linens

Oriental Gifts and Products
96 Bayard St.
New York, NY 10013
212.608.6670
paper lanterns, sandalwood fans

Palais Royal
1725 Braodway St.
Charlottesville, VA 22902
800.207.5207
linens; call for local availability

Paper White Ltd.
Fairfax, CA
415.457.7673
linens, lace

Party Tables
nationwide
800.767.8901
linens

Simon Pearce
120 Wooster St.
New York, NY 10012
800.774.5277
212.334.2393
www.simonpearceglass.com
gifts

Rayon Vert
3187 16th St.
San Francisco, CA 94103
415.861.3516
home accessories, linens, furniture,
flowers

Room Service
4354 Lovers Lane
Dallas, TX 75225
214.369.7666
home accessories, vintage finds,
furniture, design services

Room with a View
1600 Montana Ave.
Santa Monica, CA 90403
310.453.7009
www.roomview.com
linens

Rue de France
800.777.0998
housewares, gifts

Deborah Schenck
42 Kibling Hill Rd.
Stratford, VT 05072
802.765.9605
www.deborahschenck.com
framed artwork, decorative objects

**Seibert & Rice Fine
Italian Terracotta**
Short Hills, NJ
973.467.8266
www.seibert-rice.com
terracotta containers; catalog

Sferra Brothers
77 Cliffwood Ave.
Cliffwood, NJ 07721
732.290.2230
www.sferra.com
linens

Slips
1534 Grant St.
San Francisco, CA 94133
415.362.5652
custom fabrications, slipcovers

Jana Starr Antiques
236 East 80th St.
New York, NY 10021
212.861.8256
914.664.6050
antique linens and accessories

Tiffany & Co.
727 Fifth Ave.
New York, NY 10022
212.755.8000

Treillage
418 East 75th St.
New York, NY 10021
212.535.2288
garden ornaments, weathered
furniture, accessories

Trousseau Fine Vintage Linens
219 Royal Poinciana Way, #2
Palm Beach, FL 33480
561.832.9696
561.602.7571

Tudor Rose Antiques
28 E. Tenth St.
New York, NY 10003
212.677.5239
decorative silver

Urban Archaeology
285 Lafayette St.
New York, NY 10012
212.431.6969
garden architectural objects;
for purchase or rent

Vertu
4514 Travis Rd., Suite 125
Dallas, TX 75205
214.520.7817
www.vertuonline.com
fine china, flatware; registry

Wedding List Company
41 East 11th St.
New York, NY 10003
800.877.WEDLIST
212.331.1190
www.theweddinglist.com
gifts; bridal registry

Carla Weisburg
New York, NY
212.620.5276
custom textile design, table linens,
pillows

White Linen
520 Bedford Rd.
Pleasantville, NY 10570
800.828.0269
914.769.4551

**Brian Windsor Art, Antiques,
Garden Furnishings**
272 Lafayette St.
New York, NY 10003
212.274.0411

Men's Fashions

A.B.A. Tuxedo
520 S. Archer
Chicago, IL 60632
773.585.9777

Alfred Dunhill
201 N. Rodeo Dr.
Beverly Hills, CA 90210
310.274.5351

Ascot Chang
7 West 57th St.
New York, NY 10019
212.759.3333
9551 Wilshire Blvd.
Beverly Hills, CA 90211
301.550.1339

Black Tie
1 Daniel Burnham Court,
San Francisco, CA 94109
415.346.9743
www.blacktietuxedos.com

Brooks Brothers
346 Madison Ave.
New York, NY 10017
212.682.8800
416 N. Park Center
Dallas, TX 75225
214.363.2196
201 Post St.
San Francisco, CA 94108
415.397.4500
www.brooksbrothers.com

Carrot & Gibbs
1700 38th St.
Boulder, CO 80301
303.449.2821
www.carrot-gibbs.com
silk bow ties, how-to-tie brochure;
call for local availability

D'Alesio Tuxedos
333 E. Camelback Rd.
Phoenix, AZ 85012
602.265.4431

Gianfranco Ferre
270 N. Rodeo Dr.
Beverly Hills, CA 90210
310.273.6311

A.T. Harris Formalwear
11 East 44th St.
New York, NY 10017
212.682.6325

Louis, Boston
234 Berkeley St.
Boston, MA 02116
800.225.5135
www.louisboston.com
formalwear, suitings made to order

Gene Meyer
730 Fifth Ave., 12th Floor
New York, NY 10019
212.980.0110
silk ties; call for local availability

Mr. Tuxedo
Cincinatti, Ohio
513.281.2400

Mitchell's Formal Wear
377 Hickory Ridge Mall
Memphis, TN 38115
901.795.7607
www.formalfun.com

Paul Smith
108 Fifth Ave.
New York, NY 10011
212.627.9770
www.paulsmith.co.uk.com

Polo/Ralph Lauren
867 Madison Ave.
New York, NY 10021
212.606.2100
444 N. Rodeo Dr.
Beverly Hills, CA 90210
310.281.7200
58 Highland Park Village
Dallas, TX 75205
214.522.5270
90 Post St.
San Francisco, CA 94102
415.788.7656

Saks Fifth Avenue West
9600 Wilshire Blvd.
Beverly Hills, CA 90212
310.275.4211

Shanghai Tang
667 Madison Ave.
New York, NY 10021
212.888.0111
www.shanghaitang.com

Sulka
430 Park Ave.
New York, NY 10022
212.980.5200
255 Post St.
San Francisco, CA 94108
415.989.0600
262 N. Rodeo Dr.
Beverly Hills, CA 90210
310.859.9940
accessories; catalog

Terrence Teng
New York, NY
212.772.1519
silk vests; custom design available

Tux & Tails
4627 E. Cactus Rd.
Phoenix, AZ 85032
602.996.3321
18 locations

Tuxedo Center
7360 Sunset Blvd.
Hollywood, CA 90046
323.874.4200

Valentino
New York, NY
212.772.6969
Beverly Hills, CA
310.247.0103

Whittier Tux
11214 E. Whittier Blvd.
Whittier, CA 90606
562.699.2662

Wilkes Bashford Company
375 Sutter St.
San Francisco, CA 94108
415.986.4380

Worth & Worth
331 Madison Ave.
New York, NY 10017
212.867.6058
collapsible silk top hats,
fur felt bowlers

Music

Adler Entertainment
8608 Ellen Court
Baltimore, MD 21234
888.ADLERDJ
410.668.5572

Melissa Anderson, Harpist
Chicago, IL
312.360.9017

Baguette Quartet
San Francisco, CA
510.528.3723

Liz and Jack Bert String Quartet
8817 Interlake
Interlochen, MI 49643
616.276.9020

Gerard Carelli Orchestra
New York, New Jersey, and
Connecticut
800.GC.SINGS
212.989.4042

Celebration Consultants
2400 E. Oakton St., Suite 103
Arlington Heights, IL 60005
847.718.0225
by appointment

CTO
New York, NY
212.604.9025
Philadelphia, PA
610.688.8866

Curtis Music & Entertainment
Elizabeth, NJ
908.532.3131
string, brass, woodwind ensembles,
orchestras, and chamber groups

Danoff String Quartet
271 South 15th St.; #1404
Philadelphia, PA 19102
215.545.3915

Desert Chamber Musicians
4120 N. Marshall Way, Suite 3
Scottsdale, AZ 85251
602.949.8739

Divertimento Music
Marianne Carefoot
785 Windermere Ave.
Toronto, ON M6S 3M5
416.769.8685

Alex Donner Entertainment
nationwide
800.ITS.MUSIC
orchestras, various sizes

Peter Duchin Orchestras
60 East 42nd St., 15th Floor
New York, NY 10017
212.972.2260

Entertainment Connection
1202 Lincoln Ave., Suite 101
San Jose, CA 95125
408.275.6325

Bob Fangmeyer, DJ
Cincinatti, OH
513.521.4410

Festival Brass
1324 Highland Rd.
Dallas, TX 75218
214.328.9330
www.keathlywebs/fbrass.htm
classical musicians, singer; all brass
instruments

Four Voices String Quartet
3452 45th Ave.
Minneapolis, MN 55406
612.724.3591

Georgia Frances Orchestra
201 Wesley St.
Oak Park, IL 60302
708.386.8568

Harry Hershey Orchestra
22275 Harvest Oval
Strongsville, OH 44136
440.238.1138

Sam Kimball Sounds
New York, NY
212.465.9114
full-service music broker, house band,
reggae, rock, swing, chamber, DJ

Ladies Choice String Quartet
Los Angeles, CA
310.391.3762

La Folia Chamber Ensemble
Los Angeles, CA
818.761.5560

Hank Lane Orchestra
New York, NY
212.767.0600
www.hanklane.com
orchestras, vocals, swing, rock, standards

Lester Lanin
New York, NY
212.265.5208
orchestras, vocals, swing, rock, standards

Magnolia Jazz Band
Sunnyvale, CA
408.245.9120
www.magnoliajazz.com

Majestic Brass
Holbrook, NY
516.472.5363

Manhattan Swing Orchestras
244 West 54th St., Suite 604
New York, NY 10019
212.765.8850

Morgan's Disc Jockey Service
739 Albert St.
Oshawa, ON L1H 4T7
905.432.1791
www.ricmorgan@cdia.org

Music by Request
533 Montpelier Court
Fort Wright, KY 41011
606.331.3866

Preferred Artists
Ridgefield, CT
800.477.8558
artists' representative; swing, R&B

Carrie Rothenberger
Santa Monica, CA
310.452.7878
professional singer, duet artist
available upon request

**Marcom Savoy and the
Hurricanes**
San Francisco, CA
415.331.3539

**Steve Somers Band with
Valerie Barrymore**
Ypsilanti, MI
734.487.1977

Special Touch DJ Services
6405 Tyne Ave.
Cincinatti, OH 45213
513.631.1338

Spin 'n' Dance
516 N. Milwaukee Ave.
Wheeling, IL 60090
847.537.8211

**Sterling String Quartet &
Sterling Music Ensembles**
New York, NY
212.481.7697
classical ensembles, harp, flute,
classical guitar

**Sterling Trio—Flute, Violin,
and Cello**
San Francisco, CA
510.524.2569

Swing Fever
San Francisco, CA
415.459.2428
www.swingfever.com

Totally Entertainment
8715 La Tijera Blvd.
Los Angeles, CA 90045
310.665.1620

Willow Productions
13 Haviland St.
Boston, MA 02115
617.421.9336
www.willow-entertainment.com

Doug Winters Music
400 King St.
Chappaqua, NY 10514
914.238.9100

World Entertainment
New York & Philadelphia
212.604.9025

Photographers

Absolute Photography
Eden Prairie, MN
612.906.7626

**Absolute Photography/
Videography**
Woodland Hills, CA
818.774.0065
www.absolutephotovideo.com

**Arizona Wedding
Photography**
Mesa, AZ
602.641.7403

Artistic Video Productions
Houston, TX
713.526.6874
www.artisticvideo.com

Augeson Photography
St. Paul, MN
612.753.4072

Avalon Photography
Denver, CO
303.840.1324

**Babboni's Creative Image
Photography**
Wisconsin
800.807.7701
414.328.3211
call for appointment and studio hours

Bachrach Photographs
Boston, MA
617.536.4730
formal portraits

Bachrach Studio
New York, NY
212.755.6233
formal portraits

Doris Barnes
Manhattan & Woodstock, NY
212.505.5487
914.679.9323

Jim Bastardo
New York, NY
718.625.1205

Jenny Bissell
Cleveland, OH
440.247.7988

Susan Bloch
Huntington, NY
516.549.0203
black and white and color

Jamie Bosworth Photography
Portland, OR
503.246.5378

Kaija Berzins Braus
New York, NY
212. 226.3661
www.kaija.com
call for appointment

**Bride Keep the Negatives
Wedding Photography**
Seattle, WA
206.367.6388

Joe Buissink
Beverly Hills, CA
310.360.0198

Hilary N. Bullock Photography
Minneapolis, MN
612.338.7516

Robert Caddick Photographers
Baltimore, MD
800.238.2147

Candid Wedding Photographers
Phoenix, AZ
602.242.8444

Jack Caputo
Brentwood, CA
310.476.8825

Philippe Cheng
New York, NY
212.627.4262

Tom Chute
Indianapolis, IN
317.849.5377

Stephane Colbert
Sandy Hook, CT
203.426.0448
212.366.4407
www.stephanecolbert.com

Leslie Corrado Photographer
San Francisco, CA
415.431.3917
www.lesliecorrado.com

Coughlin Studio
Tinley Park, IL
708.633.7344
www.coughlinstudio.com

Maureen Edwards DeFries
Brookfield, CT
203.740.9343
www.maureenedwardsdefries.com
portraits, custom albums

**Genevieve de Manio
Photography**
Boston, MA
617.661.8760
black and white journalistic
photography

John Derryberry Photography
Dallas, TX
214.357.5457
www.johnderryberry.com
black and white; custom albums

Barry P. Dowe Photography
Lake Villa, IL
847.356.8136
www.lakecountrybusiness.com

Ets-Hokin Studios
San Francisco, CA
415.695.0600
www.etshokin.com

**Focus Pocus Photography
& Video**
Phoenix, AZ
602.331.1813

**Michelle Frankfurter
Photography**
Washington, DC
202.462.0028
black and white documentary style

Rob Fraser
New York, NY
212.941.0433
black and white documentary style;
portraits

Robert Friedel
New York, NY
212.477.3452
color and black and white

GBV Productions
Philadelphia, PA
800.305.7226

Robert George
St. Louis, MO
314.771.6622
www.robertgeorgestudio.com
color and black and white

Grevy Photography
New Orleans, LA
504.866.5093
portraits

Steven E. Gross
Chicago, IL
773.509.9398
black and white a specialty

Gruber Photographers
New York, NY
212.262.9777
black and white a specialty

Greg Harring, Photojournalist
Boulder, CO
303.245.8025
www.gregharring.com

Cary Hazlegrove Photography
Austin, TX
888.474.9673
512.452.6181
www.hazlegrove.com
color and black and white

David Hechler at Harold Hechler & Assoc.
New York, NY
212.472.6565
call for appointment

Heirloom Restoration
New Haven, CT
203.795.0565
photographic restoration; appraisal by mail

Joyce Heisen Casual Candids
Washington Crossing, PA
800.982.7774
215.493.6792
photojournalistic style

Nelson Hume
New York, NY
212.222.7424
videography and editing services

Anthony Israel Photography
New York, NY
718.387.4886
photojournalistic style

Jim Johnson Photography
Washington, DC
202.686.7300
www.picturestorystudio

Cheryl Klauss
New York, NY
212.431.3569

Yorghos Kontaxis
Brooklyn, NY
718.491.3705

Phil Kramer Photography
Philadelphia, PA
215.928.9189
www.philkramerphoto.com

Tanya Malott Lawson
787.721.1232
www.photographybytanya.com
worldwide weddings, portraits, children; color and black and white

Tamantha Lewis Photography
Lawrenceville, GA
770.237.5141
www.tlphoto.simplenet.com

Michael Lichterman
Clifford Norton Studio
Lyndhurst, OH
440.646.0800

Longshots Photography
New Orleans, LA
504.282.3559
www.georgelong.com

Frank Lopez
Dallas, TX
877.321.5411
214.321.5411
www.franklopez.com
black and white journalistic photographs

Christopher Lowry Photography
Cincinatti, OH
513.221.3233

Fred Marcus Photography
New York, NY
212.873.5588
www.weddingcentral.com/ny/fmarcus
formal portraits, videography

Mia Matheson
New York, NY
212.721.0808
www.matheson.com

Richard Mayer Photography
San Francisco, CA
650.508.1201

Sarah Merians Photography
New York, NY
212.633.0502
www.sarahmerians.com

Moment in Time Video
Aurora, CO
303.400.0525

Clifford Norton Studio
Lyndhurst, OH
440.646.0800
www.cliffordnorton.com

Mary O'Toole Photography
Boston, Nantucket, New York
888.665.0472

Luciana Pampalone
New York, NY
212.564.2883

Alan Parker Photography
Toronto, ON
416.282.3142

Michelle Pattee
Mill Valley, CA
415.773.8188
www.photography@michellepattee.com

Photo Sensations
Vancouver, BC
604.731.2348

Mike Posey Photography and Video
New Orleans, LA
504.488.8000
also videography

Professional Photographers of America
Atlanta, GA
888.97.STORY
www.ppa_world.com

Denis Reggie Photography
Atlanta, GA
800.379.1999
404.817.8080
photojournalistic style

Reportage
Toronto, ON
416.461.6617

Curtis Rhodes Wedding Photography
Seattle, WA
206.782.3681
www.isomedia.com/homes/crhodes

Jeannie Frey Rhodes
Baton Rouge, LA
225.927.8282
black and white a specialty

Robin Sachs Photography
Dallas, TX
214.824.0624
color and black and white;
portraits only

Mallory Samson
New York, NY and Sausalito, CA
212.673.0668
415.332.3696

Cynthia Schick Designs
nationwide
973.746.5582
hand-painting of black and white
photographs

Corinne Schippert Photography
Arlington, MA
781.643.1919
www.shippertphotography.com

Wendi Schneider
Denver, CO
303.322.2246
portraits, Polaroid transfers,
hand-painted images

Sengbush Photography
Dallas, TX
214.363.3264

Valerie Shaff
New York, NY
212.965.1080

Karen Simmons & Associates
Atlanta, GA
404.814.7773

Julie Skarratt Photography
New York, NY
212.877.2604

Hal Slifer
Boston, MA
800.234.7755
617.787.7910
videography

Smash Box Studio
Culver City, CA
310.558.7660
photography studios

Special Touch Photography
Cincinatti, OH
513.631.1338

Stephen Photography
Louisville, KY
502.244.3753

William Stites
Marathon, FL
305.743.6455

Supreme Video Works
Tony Arzt
Connecticut
203.938.9161
videographer and filmmaker; by
appointment

John Tilley Photography
Dallas, TX
214.358.4747
also portraits

Tanya Tribble
New York, NY
212.255.5275
nontraditional photography

Keith Trumbo
New York, NY
212.580.7104
color and black and white

John Unrue Photography
Winter Park, FL
407.629.5292
www.unruephoto.com

Jason Walz Photography
Brooklyn, NY
718.596.9081

**Priscilla Wannamaker
Photographer**
Atlanta, GA
404.261.1003
www.pwannamaker.com

**Wedding & Event
Videographers Association
International**
Sarasota, FL
800.501.9382
www.weva.com

Wedlock Photography
Vancouver, B.C.
604.689.5442
www.wedlockphotography.com

Marlene Wetherell
New York, NY
212.877.3071

Ross Whitaker
New York, NY
212.279.2600
www.rosswhitaker.com
color and black and white; also
videography

Joyce Wilson
Indianapolis, IN
317.786.1769

John Wolfsohn
Beverly Hills, CA
310.859.9266

Zalewa Image Designers
Georgetown, IN
800.836.7688
812.951.3259
502.451.0307

Signs/Calligraphy/ Stationery

Marjorie Parrot Adams
Lancaster, MA
978.368.4225
fine paper

T. Anthony
445 Park Ave.
New York, NY 10022
800.722.2406
212.750.9797
leather albums; catalog

Arch
407 Jackson St.
San Francisco, CA 94133
415.433.2724
albums, journals

Helen Aulisa
75 Hudson St.
New York, NY 10013
212.267.6471
handmade cards

Stephannie Barba
432 East 88th St., Suite 401
New York, NY 10028
212.426.8949
custom design; illustrations;
wedding stationery with
hand-painted flowers a specialty

Blue Marmalade
1500 Jackson St. NE
Minneapolis, MN 55413
612.788.8517
computer-generated calligraphy,
whimsical invitations

BOHO Designs
San Francisco, CA
415.441.1617
custom invitations

Gail Brill Design
333 Valley Rd.
Cos Cob, CT 06807
203.869.4667
by appointment

William Ernest Brown Stationers
Dallas, TX
214.891.0008

Calligraphy by Christy
1721 N. Daffodil St.
Tempe, AZ 85281
602.720.8207

Calligraphy by Margie
4661 Forest St. SE
Mercer Island, WA 98040
206.232.7343

Calligraphy Design Studio
711 Kessler Blvd. West
Indianapolis, IN 46228
317.257.6968

Barbara Callow Calligraphy
1686 Union St., Suite 204
San Francisco, CA 94123
415.928.3303

Campbell Stationers & Engravers
8407 Pickwick Lane
Dallas, TX 75225
214.692.8380

Center for Book Arts
28 West 27th St., 3rd Floor
New York, NY 10001
212.460.9768
bookbinding; call for referrals, classes

Chapman Calligraphy & Lettering
Xenia, OH
937.372.3283

Nancy Sharon Collins Stationer
New York, NY
888.431.5959
212.431.5959
hand-engraved stationery

David Copperfield's Stationers
254 W. Portal Ave.
San Francisco, CA 94127
415.681.5040
calligraphy

Cordially Yours
Newton Center, MA 02459
617.969.6048
invitations, calligraphy, accessories

Crane & Company
800.IS.CRANE
call for local availability;
publishes Crane's Blue Book
(invitation etiquette)

Dieu Donne Papermill
433 Broome St.
New York, NY 10013
212.266.0573
www.colophon.com/dieudonne
custom handmade papers,
monograms, watermarks

Empire Stamp & Seal
36 East 29th St.
New York, NY 10016
212.679.5370
blind embosses, custom rubber stamps

Flax Art & Design
1699 Market St.
San Francisco, CA 94103
800.547.7778
415.552.2355
sign-making supplies

Anna Griffin Design
490 Armour Circle
Atlanta, GA 30324
404.817.8170
www.annagriffin.com
stationery

Gump's
135 Post Rd.
San Francisco, CA 94108
415.982.1616

Judy Ivry
25 East 4th St., #2
New York, NY 10003
212.677.1015
embossed albums; by appointment

Cheryl Jacobsen Calligraphy and Design
1131 E. Burlington St.
Iowa City, IA 52240
319.351.6603
calligraphy; call for consultaion

Jam Paper
611 Avenue of the Americas
New York, NY 10011
212.255.4593
www.jampaper.com
card, paper stock, envelopes

J&M Martinez Graphique de France
9 State St.
Woburn, MA 01801
800.444.1464
www.graphiquedefrance.com
letterpress stationery, journals;
call for local availability

Kate's Paperie
561 Broadway
New York, NY 10012
212.941.9816
8 West 13th St.
New York, NY 10011
212.633.0570
handmade papers, albums, custom
invitations

K2 Design
Dallas, TX
214.522.2344
calligraphy

Claudia Laub Studio
7404 Beverly Blvd.
Los Angeles, CA 90036
323.931.1710
letterpress, custom designs; catalog

Lee's Art Shop
220 West 57th St.
New York, NY 10019
212.247.0110
sign-making supplies

Lettering Design Group
5830 Nall Ave.
Mission, KS 66202
913.362.7864
ornamental penmanship

Carole Maurer
Wynnewood, PA
610.642.9726
calligraphy; call for consultation

Barbara Mauriello
231 Garden St.
Hoboken, NJ 07030
201.420.6613
hand bookbinding; by appointment

Heather Belle McQuale
210 Douglas Ave.
Charlottesville, VA 22902
804.923.8888
script styles, illustrated details

Claire Mendelson
New York, NY
416.784.1426
custom-made ketubot

Rae Michaels Ltd.
521 Madison Ave.
New York, NY 10022
212.688.2256
custom inivitations; by appointment

Mill Valley Art Materials
433 Miller Ave.
Mill Valley, CA 94941
415.388.5642
sign-making supplies

New York Central Art Supply
62 Third Ave.
New York, NY 10003
800.950.6111
www.nycentralart.com
sign-making supplies

Paper Access
23 West 18th St.
New York, NY 10011
212.463.7035
papers, embossing supplies; catalog

Paper Garden
555 W. Bitters Rd.
San Antonio, TX 78216
210.494.9602
stationery, rubber stamps

Papermarché
3471A Yonge St.
Toronto, ON M4N 2N3
416.487.9538
www.papermarche.com
fine papers, custom invitations

Paper Place
4001 N. Lamar Blvd.
Austin, TX 78756
512.451.6531
www.paperplaceaustin.invitations.com
stationery, fine papers

Paper Routes
404 Exposition Ave.
Dallas, TX 75226
214.828.9494
handmade papers

Papineau Calligraphy
5772 Thornhill Dr.
Oakland, CA 94611
510.339.2301
by appointment

Papyrus
800.872.7978
www.papyrusstores.com
custom invitations, announcements,
stationery, calligraphy

Pearl Paint
308 Canal St.
New York, NY 10013
www.pearlpaint.com
sign-making supplies

Pendragon, Ink
27 Prospect St.
Whitinsville, MA 01588
508.234.6843
hand-lettered, hand-painted stationery

Prose & Letters
351 Brookwood Dr.
San Jose, CA 95116
408.293.1852
calligraphy

Purgatory Pie Press
19 Hudson St., # 403
New York, NY 10013
212.274.8228
www.purgatorypiepress.com
custom hand-set type, albums, letterpress, stationery; by appointment

**Janet Redstone Fine
Calligraphy & Design**
316 Delta Rd.
Highland Park, IL 60035
312.944.6624
custom monograms; brochure
available; by appointment

Renaissance Writings
800.246.8483
www.renaissancewritings.com

**Rose Leaves Calligraphy &
Invitations**
5911 Chatsworth Lane
Bethesda, MD 20814
301.493.5554

Paula Rubenstein
37500 Jackson Rd.
Chagrin Falls, OH 44022
440.247.1906
716.789.4712
stationery with antique lace motif

Ruffles & Flourishes
Richland, WA
509.627.5906
blind embossing, molded paper stationery; call for local availability

Sam Flax
12 West 20th St.
New York, NY 10003
212.431.7932
1460 Northside Dr.
Atlanta, GA 30318
404.352.7200
1401 E. Colonial Dr.
Orlando, FL 32803
407.898.9785
sign-making supplies

Evelyn Schramm
Dallas, TX
972.612.8232
calligraphy

Angela Scott
Sag Harbor, NY
516.537.3918
bookbinder; custom album design

Silberman-Brown Stationer
1322 Fifth Ave.
Seattle, WA 98101
206.292.9404

SoHo Letterpress
71 Greene St.
New York, NY 10012
212.334.4357
custom stationery, printing, graphic
design, letterpress

Soolip Paperie & Press
8646 Melrose Ave.
West Hollywood, CA 90069
310.360.0545

**Mrs. John L. Strong Fine
Stationery**
New York, NY
212.838.3775
hand engraving; by appointment

Studio Z Mendocino
711 N. Main St.
Fort Bragg, CA 95437
707.964.9448
letterpress stationery; call for local availability

Tail of the Yak
2632 Ashby Ave.
Berkeley, CA 94705
510.841.9891
invitations, accessories

Tiffany & Co.
727 Fifth Ave.
New York, NY 10022
212.755.8000
210 N. Rodeo Dr.
Beverly Hills, CA 90210
310.273.8880
350 Post Rd.
San Francisco, CA 94108
415.781.7000
13350 Dallas Parkway, Suite 1020
Dallas, TX 75240
214.458.2800
www.tiffany.com
invitations

Two Women
1108 Howard St.
San Francisco, CA 94103
800.322.1979
415.431.8805
paper gifts; call for local availability

Two Women Boxing
Dallas, TX
214.939.1626
silkscreen journals and gifts; call for local availability

Washington Engraving Company
1430 H St., NW
Washington, DC 20005
202.638.3100
www.washengr@erols.com
invitations, imported papers

Sharon Watts
Brooklyn, NY
718.398.0451
calligraphy, illustrations, artwork

Ellen Weldon Design
273 Church St.
New York, NY 10013
212.925.4483
engraving, printing, calligraphy; by appointment

Write Selection
314 Preston Royal Center
Dallas, TX 75230
214.750.0531

Zorn Design Studio
1800 Diamond Ave.
Pasadena, CA 91030
323.344.9995

Tent and Party Rentals

AA Party Rentals
6404 216 St., SW
Mountlake Terrace, WA 98043
425.640.5547
candelabras, candles, kneeling benches, columns, canopies, tableware

Abbey Party Rentals
1310 North 131st St.
Seattle, WA 98133
800.89.ABBEY

Abbey Party Rents
Robert Slavik
2525 W. Mockingbird Lane
Dallas, TX 75235
214.350.5373

ABC Rental
8801 Belair Rd.
Baltimore, MD 21236
410.256.3670

ABC Rental Center
10 North 2nd St.
Laurel, MD 20707
301.498.2991
lawn and garden, tents, chairs, tables, fountains

Affairs Party Rental
6140 Ordan Dr.
Mississauga, ON L5T 2B3
905.795.1600

Alpine Equipment & Party Rental
8121 Broadway
Lemon Grove, CA
619.460.RENT
tents

American Party Rentals
3633 S. Allston Ave.
Durham, NC 27713
919.544.1555
www.americanpartyrentals.com
tabletop, chairs, linens, tents

American Party Rentals
921 E. War Memorial Dr.
Peoria, IL 61614
309.688.1412
tabletop, tents, canopies, linens, staging, dance floors

American Rental Association
800.334.2177
national referral service; party rental brochures

A Plus Rental Center
7701 Fullerton Rd.
Springfield, VA 22153
703.451.6060
www.aplusrental.com

Arizona Party Rental
4826 E. Speedway Blvd.
Tuscon, AZ 85712
www.azparty.qpg.com
canopies, portable bars, lighting heating, cooking, candelabras

Atlanta Tent Rental
Roswell, GA
770.667.2555

A to Z Rentals
3550 Cedar Ave. South
Minneapolis, MN 55407
612.729.2231

Austin Rent All
9402-A United Dr.
Austin, TX 78758
888.21.PARTY
512.491.7368
www.austinrentall.com

Ballroom Elegance
18321 NE 19th Ave.
Miami, FL 33179
305.936.0669
www.ballroomelegance.com
linens

BBJ Linen
7855 Grosse Point Rd.
Skokie, MI 60077
800.722.0126
248.722.0216
nationwide

**Bentley Meeker Lighting
& Staging**
New York, NY
212.722.3349
www.bentleymeeker.com

Be Our Guest Rentals
24 Blue Hill Ave.
Boston, MA 2119
617.427.2700

Bergen Rentals
Elmwood Park
201.796.9280
www.bergenrentals.com
tents, tables, chairs

Better Rents
14951 Moran
Westminster, CA 92683
714.891.5522
candelabras, wooden archways, tabletop

Big 4 Rents
5500 Commerce Blvd.
Berkeley, CA 94710
510.559.4444

**Blood's Seafood, Catering &
Party Rentals**
1147 Hartford Ave.
White River Jcy., VT 05001
802.295.9287
www.bloodsseafood.com
tents, chairs, linens

**Capron Lighting &
Sound Company**
278 West St.
Needham, MA 02494
781.444.8850

Celebrations Unlimited
40 E. Bacon
Hillsdale, MI
517.439.9810
decorative items

Charlie's Rental Center
2168 Washington Rd.
Washington, IL 61571
309.688-1412
tabletop, linens, staging, dance floors,
tents, canopies

Classic Party Rentals
8476 Steller Dr.
Culver City, CA 90232
310.202.0011

Colonial Party Rental
2775 Bond St.
Detroit, MI 48309
248.853.9244

Creative Tables
408 S. Atlanta St., Suite 140
Atlanta, GA 30075
770.992.1113
specialty linens

**Ducky Bob's Cannonball
Party Rentals**
Carrollton, TX
972.381.8000
party supplies, tents

East Peoria Rentals
2246 E. Washington St.
East Peoria, IL 61611
309.694.3465
chairs

Eureka Tent Rentals
2701 W. Britton Rd.
Oklahoma City, OK 73120
405.751.3100
www.eurekatents.com

Fiesta Tents
1575 50th Ave.
Lachine, Quebec H8T 3C8
514.636.9333
www.fiesta.ca

Fillamento
2185 Fillmore St.
San Francisco, CA 94115
415.931.2224
candles

First Class Party Rentals
11215 1st. Ave.
Whittier, CA 90603
800.727.8992
562.902.7535

Ruth Fischl
141 West 28th St.
New York, NY 10001
212.273.9710
www.ruthfischl.com
linens, decorative accessories

Fox Tent & Awning Company
617 S. Ashley St.
Ann Arbor, MI 48104
734.665.9126

Frost Lighting
1880 W. Fullerton St.
Northbrook, IL 60614
708.729.8200
full-service lighting, special effects

Grand Rental Station
1006 S. Washington Ave.
Holland, MI 49423
616.396.7300
tents, banquet facility

Just Linens
New York, NY
212.688.8808
linens; full-service rentals

Kirby Rentals Service
411 Hames Ave.
Orlando, FL 32805
800.446.1011
407.422.1000
www.kirbytent.com

David Landis Design
208 West 29th St., Room 613
New York, NY 10001
212.563.7568
www.davidlandisdesign.com
crystal candlestick bobeches; catalog;
call for local availability

Market, The
3433 W. Seventh St.
Fort Worth, TX 76107
817.334.0330
www.themarketonline.com
candles

Marketplace
245 West 29th St.
New York, NY 10012
212.594.8289
candelabras, crystal

Elizabeth Merideth
Petaluma, CA
707.763.1532
decorative wedding accessories,
lighting, call for local availability

**Monstrey's, Special Event
Professionals**
8332 E. Bingham Rd.
Traverse City, MI 49684
616.946.0018
tents, chairs, tables

Party Rental
780 W. Main St.
Watertown, NY 13601
315.788.5097
www.1000-island.net/Party/Rentals
china, linens, tables, chairs,

Party Rental Ltd.
888.774.4276
full service rentals; New York to
Virginia

Partytime Rentals
1212 S. Range Line Rd.
Carmel, IN 46032
317.844.5178
www.partytime-rental.com

Partytime Tents & Canopies
Branchville, NJ
973.948.2426

Perfect Party Rental
7810 E. Pierce St.
Scottsdale, AZ 85257
602.994.0681
tents, canopies, event planning

Peterson Party Center
139 Swanton St.
Winchester, MA 01890
781.729.4000
www.ppcinc.com
full-service rentals

Rent a Party
1924 Yajome
Napa, CA 94559
707.252-7368
tents, canopies

Rents Unlimited
4324 W. Northern
Glendale, AZ 85301
602.931.2469

Ryan Productions
13 Revere St.
Jamaica Plain, MA 02130
617.522.3339
lighting, technical design, sound

Service Party Rentals
770 Lexington Ave., 11th Floor
New York, NY
212.288.7384
linens, dishes, silverware

**Stamford Tents &
Party Rental**
54 Research Dr.
Stamford, CT 06901
203.324.6222

Stortz Lighting
70 Laight St., 1st floor
New York, NY 10021
212.219.2330
full-service lighting, special effects

Sugarplum Tent Company
16610 Sugarland Rd.
Boyds, MD 20841
301.869.2054
www.sugarplumtents.com

Summer House
21 Throckmorton Ave.
Mill Valley, CA 94941
415.383.6695

Tabletoppers
450-B Lake Cook Rd.
Deerfield, IL 60015
800.826.9576

Taylor Rental-Party Plus
274 Broad St.
Manchester, CT 06040
860.643.2496
weddings; greater central
Connecticut

Vermont Tent Company
14 Berard Ave,
South Burlington, VT 05403
800.696.TENT
www.vtevent.com/tent.htm
tents, stages, dance floors;
Connecticut, Massachuesetts, and
New Hampshire

Watts Up!
1237 N. Vine St.
Hollywood, CA 90058
323.465.2000

Weaver's Rent-All
212 N. Main
Normal, IL 61761
309.452.RENT
everything including tool rental

Wedding Details
6671 East M72
Williamsburg, MI 49690
800.44.TENTS
www.weddingdetails.com/tents
tents

J.G. Willis, Inc.
Keith Waters
Boston, MA
617.527.0037
tents